THE
PASSIONATE
COLLECTOR

Books by Roy R. Neuberger

So Far, So Good: The First 94 Years

An autobiography by Roy R. Neuberger
with Alfred and Roma Connable

THE
PASSIONATE
COLLECTOR

Eighty Years in the World of Art

ROY R. NEUBERGER

With Alfred and Roma Connable

 JOHN WILEY & SONS, INC.

For general information on our other products and services, or technical support, please
contact our Customer Care Department within the United States at (800) 762-2974,
outside the United States at (317) 572-3993, or fax (317) 572-4002.

Wiley also publishes its books in a variety of electronic formats. Some content that
appears in print may not be available in electronic books.

For more information about Wiley products, visit our web site at www.wiley.com.

ISBN 0-471-27343-0

Printed in the United States of America.

10   9   8   7   6   5   4   3   2   1

This book is dedicated with great affection and respect to the extraordinary, original, passionate artists who have enriched my life beyond measure.

THE
PASSIONATE
COLLECTOR

CONTENTS

Portrait on wall by Peter Fink. (Photo by Fran Sotnick.)

PREFACE

My interest in art began when I was an eighteen-year-old college drop-out, working at the B. Altman department store and
taking art lessons at night. I decided that I would never be a first-
rate painter. But I discovered that I loved art and had a good eye
for it.

Later, living in Paris in the 1920s, I read Floret Fels' compelling
biography of Vincent van Gogh, who had died in torment and

poverty. He was one of the greatest artists of all time, and no one would buy his paintings.

The French flunked with van Gogh and Paul Cezanne, who was not given a one-man show until he was fifty-six. Even then, the reviews were tepid. When Cezanne died in 1906, he had no idea that the world would view him as a great painter.

I wanted America to do better by its artists. I resolved to collect the work of living artists and to encourage others to do the same.

In retrospect, this was an audacious decision for a young man of modest means and no career. I returned to America from Paris and went to work on Wall Street because, as the celebrated safecracker Willie Sutton replied when asked why he robbed banks, "That's where the money is." Fortunately, I did well on Wall Street without robbing any banks.

I was a trainee at the Wall Street firm of Halle and Stieglitz on Black Tuesday, October 29, 1929. Older, wiser, and richer men lost millions, but I came out of the Panic intact and with a greater appreciation of the vagaries of the market.

The firm I founded in 1939, Neuberger & Berman, where I still enjoy going to work, now manages $55 billion of other people's money. Success on Wall Street enabled me to buy more than a thousand works of art from gifted painters and sculptors, and to become an art advocate and activist. Some of the paintings and sculptures that I bought purely because I loved them were later critically acclaimed. I still derive enormous pleasure from a fine painting or sculpture, and I hope that at age 99 my critical and appreciative senses remain sharp.

Although I have collected art for almost eighty years, I have never sold the work of a living artist. Nelson Rockefeller, when he was governor of New York, wanted to buy my collection. I wouldn't sell. He then persuaded me to give away most of it by establishing the

Neuberger Museum of Art at Purchase College, part of the State University of New York.

Earlier, beginning in 1945 with the gift of four paintings (including a Milton Avery) to the Brooklyn Museum; then with eleven paintings to the University of Michigan; nineteen to Mount Holyoke; eight to Bryn Mawr; and other paintings to Williams, Smith, and Yale; I worked to place art in universities and museums across the country.

So far, I have given more than 950 paintings and sculptures to the Neuberger Museum, including thirty-three Averys, and 500 more to seventy other museums and colleges.

My effort, in giving away art and donating money to museums to acquire art, has been to help foster interest in the work of contemporary artists.

I am happy to have played a role in the development and acceptance of living artists. Beyond their professional lives, I have been committed to seeing that artists could pay their rent and eat a decent meal.

Helping artists and developing museums is an old tradition in the financial world. J. P. Morgan, the Mellon family, and the Rockefellers were all outstanding in creating our best museums.

The twentieth century saw a proliferation of artists in America. More people were able to live as artists than in earlier times. Americans developed much stronger reputations as important artists.

My taste in art was definitely influenced by living in Paris in the 1920s, although I wasn't aware of that until much later.

I didn't know that I was going to be a pretty well-known collector. However, I had some suspicion in 1944 when the Museum of Modern art asked me to open my home so they could view my art. I was the first person in the city they asked. By that time I had acquired Marsden Hartley's *The Fishermen's Last Supper* and several other contemporary works by breakthrough artists.

Looking at the art explosion, manifest today in the record numbers of people pouring into America's museums, I count myself fortunate to have been eyewitness and participant.

My life has been enhanced by marvelous people—museum directors and curators, collectors, dealers, critics, and art historians (including the great Meyer Schapiro, for a time my roommate in Paris), and of course the wonderful artists themselves.

For bringing me so much joy, I am grateful to Milton Avery, Jackson Pollock, Ben Shahn, Max Weber, Hans Hofmann, Alexander Calder (all of whom I collected early in their careers) as well as Henry Moore, John Marin, Edward Hopper, Willem de Kooning, Georgia O'Keeffe, and many others.

As collector, museum trustee, and president of the American Federation of Arts, I was afforded a singular window on the amazing period of American art that began about the time of the Depression and continues into the twenty-first century.

While I was buying art, traveling the country for AFA, and working with the trustees, directors, and curators of the Museum of Modern Art, the Whitney Museum of American Art, and the Metropolitan Museum of Art, the "New York School" held a commanding place in the art world. My personal world was peopled by the brilliant art professionals responsible for this glorious period of American leadership.

Outstanding scholars helped mold my taste and guide my collecting. At mid-century, an incredible group of people staffed the fine arts departments in colleges and universities and would become prime movers in America's leading museums. Among them were Francis Henry Taylor and Philippe de Montebello, both scholars before becoming directors of the Metropolitan Museum of Art; Dorothy Miller, Alfred Barr, and James Soby, all at the Museum of Modern Art; and my good friends Jack Baur and Lloyd Goodrich, both directors of the Whitney.

I rate them all highly, including Thomas Hoving, director of the Metropolitan Museum of Art for ten exciting, controversial years.

Artists, dealers, directors, curators, and collectors—these are the people who populate the pages of this book. They have enriched my life far beyond what it would have been on Wall Street alone.

I invite you to meet my friends and to share my adventures on the trail of great art.

Roy R. Neuberger and family at his eightieth birthday party in London. (Left to right standing) Ann, Roy, Marie, and Jimmy. (Sitting) Son Roy S. with youngest of Neuberger's eight grandchildren.

INTRODUCTION

Art has enriched human life for more than fifty centuries. It tells us far more about our past than we can learn from memorizing the names of kings and the dates of battles. Cave drawings, Egyptian tombs, ancient Greek plays, and Michelangelo sculptures uncover a far richer tapestry of the past then do conventional history books.

Art history has become a significant field of study at our universities. It became important at Columbia with Meyer Schapiro, at Harvard with Paul Sachs, and at the Rhode Island School of Design with Danny Robbins. Development was slower in the West but lately art and art history have assumed importance in San Francisco and Los Angeles, after a long time behind the mulberry bush.

Young people tell me that art history is a more interesting approach to learning history than more traditional courses. In art history, you learn about what was really going on in the lives of people.

Art appeals to the best and the worst of us. Some of the most terrible dictators respected art. Napoleon and Hitler liked art enough to steal it. Great treasures pilfered by Napoleon and brought to Paris are still displayed in the Louvre. Monstrous as Hitler was, he did not deliberately destroy the art he stole. Surprisingly, the watercolors he painted were not bad.

Stalin respected Russia's great museums, the Pushkin in Moscow and the Hermitage in St. Petersburg. Soviet Communists committed countless evil acts during their seventy-year run, but, unlike their Chinese counterparts, who destroyed an incalculably valuable heritage during the Cultural Revolution, the Russians had high esteem for their artistic heritage. The magnificent art of the Czars in the Hermitage and the Summer Palace was once seen only by the royal family and their friends. When Stalin took over, he opened the palaces so that all the people, not just the nobility, could enjoy Rembrandt and Velazquez.

THE AMERICAN CENTURY

America dominated the twentieth century in science, economics, finance, commerce, and the stock market. The results have been wonderful sometimes, but not always. Sometimes science made it possible for convenience to triumph over common sense. Diseases are diagnosed by MRIs and CAT scans, and cures are achieved that were never dreamed possible in my youth. We have been to the moon. The twentieth century produced radio and television, and the Internet that I don't know a thing about.

We over use the automobile and the airplane and we under use that excellent nineteenth-century phenomenon, the railroad. Something favorable seems to be happening in the development of a fast train capable of going 150 miles an hour from Washington to Boston. That is good in my opinion. I love the railroad and hate the automobile.

The revolution in medicine, including greater knowledge about diet, makes it possible for people to live at least thirty years longer than they did in the nineteenth century, and be more productive. Look at the work Picasso did in his eighties and nineties.

Two hundred years ago, George Washington died in a most ridiculous manner, after a bout with what was probably flu. They knew so little about medicine that they bled him to rid his system of the ailment. They were too efficient. They bled him to death. Today he would take one of our miracle drugs and be better in a few days.

While scientific developments were dominating the twentieth century, revolutions were occurring in the creative arts—painting, sculpture, architecture, and music. The world may not have produced another Mozart or Beethoven, but Shostakovich, Stravinsky, Rachmaninov, and Copeland are among those composers whose popularity will outlast their century. The composers and lyricists of American musicals—George and Ira Gershwin, Richard Rodgers, Larry Hart, Oscar Hammerstein, Jerome Kern, Cole Porter, Irving Berlin, and Stephen Sondheim—have given the world a great deal of pleasure.

From my perspective, starting in the 1940s, America experienced an extraordinary renaissance in the creation and appreciation of the visual arts. The art world exploded, very much the way the stock market did in the 1990s. But the bull market in art remains strong.

THE ART EXPLOSION

America produced a lot of art during the nineteenth century, much of it reasonably good, some very good. But it was unappreciated next to the European masters. In the mid-twentieth century, the United States was taken extremely seriously in the art world. Public awareness of art expanded and respect from the rest of the world for American art soared.

In America, as in Russia, millions of people now enjoy paintings and sculpture previously viewed by only a few. Imaginative museum directors have provided broad access to great art. New museums have sprung up to serve an enthusiastic public. In the early 1900s, most journalists couldn't find their way to a museum. Today, newspapers highlight the appointment of a new director and publish pictures and features on the resurgence of interest in a particular painter or sculptor.

When I first visited Washington, DC, in 1929, our nation's capital had only one exciting art museum, the Phillips Gallery. The Corcoran, which today is a a gem, was stuffy and boring. The National Gallery, part of the wonderful Smithsonian Institution developed by Andrew Mellon, was not launched for another eight years.

All across America, the art scene was dismal. Los Angeles was barren. San Francisco had three museums, but together their collections didn't add up to the importance of the Metropolitan Museum of Art. Scholarly museums existed in Philadelphia, Boston, and Chicago, but all were steadfastly devoted to the past.

In New York City, there was only the Metropolitan and the often overlooked Brooklyn Museum of Art. There was no Guggenheim, no Whitney, no Museum of Modern Art, no SoHo, and no Chelsea art scene.

The emergence of great American museums would not have been possible without highly educated directors, many of them from the academic world. Most of these people did not think of themselves as scholars, but they were. They were scholars before an expanding public forced them to become showmen.

The Museum of Modern Art acquired outstanding teachers and researchers from the Fogg Museum at Harvard and the Institute of Fine Arts in Chicago.

When the Metropolitan Museum of Art was created in 1870, it was large and stodgy. It is still the largest museum, but its growth has been accompanied by increasing quality under exciting leadership, from Francis Henry Taylor in the 1950s to Philippe de Montebello in the twenty-first century.

The first art museum in the United States was the Wadsworth Atheneum, which opened in Hartford, Connecticut, in 1842. Unlikely city, wonderful museum.

Along with the mushrooming growth of museums, there has been an explosion in art education. We know much more about the art of the Italian Renaissance than we did before, and more about ancient art. The great turn-of-the-century dealer Bernard Berenson started that. He operated from Italy but he must be credited as a powerfully influential American art scholar.

Americans love Italian art. Venice itself, a favorite of American tourists, is a work of art. When it came to fixing up a sinking Venice and flooded Florence, American scholars did most of the work. We were especially sensitive to the artistic importance of these cities.

I don't know how the twentieth century will stack up against the Italian Renaissance, or whether 100 years from now the Impressionists and Post-Impressionists will be as highly regarded as they have been for the past twenty or thirty years. The Post-Impressionists were not appreciated when I was in Paris in the 1920s. I could have bought some great French paintings, Cezanne and van Gogh, for instance, for $2,000 apiece.

MY VOW

When I vowed as a young man to collect the works of living artists, I had little idea of the richness, variety, and quality of the art that would be available to me, or of the value of friendships forged in the art world that would endure for a lifetime.

In 1997, I celebrated my ninety-fourth birthday and published a book about my career on Wall Street. But I felt that a more important task remained. Through my museum work and private collecting, I had been afforded a unique view of the twentieth-century world of American art. This carried with it, it seemed to me, a high responsibility to share some history in which I was a participant or eyewitness. And so I vowed to write this book before my 100th birthday.

Roy in his Boulevard St. Germain apartment, Paris, 1928.

CHAPTER ONE

MEMORIES OF PARIS IN THE 1920s

My years in Paris as a young man spawned my passion and my eye for art. For all the years thereafter, I gravitated with special fondness toward artists who I felt showed French, or at least European, sensibility.

I was first attracted to the work of Milton Avery because I felt that Matisse influenced him. I liked Max Weber for the same reason. My earliest important purchase, Peter Hurd's *Boy from the Plains*, reminded me of the Italian Renaissance. Lyonel Feininger's *High Houses* evoked for me early Picasso and Braque.

Paris was the dawn of my life as a passionate collector.

LINDBERGH CONQUERS PARIS

When Charles Lindbergh landed in Paris on May 21, 1927, after his solo flight across the Atlantic Ocean, I was living at 119 Boulevard St. Germain on the Left Bank.

This daring young man in his single-engine airplane, the *Spirit of St. Louis*, electrified the world. Excitement spread through the cafés of the Left Bank and all of Paris. Several hundred thousand people went to the airport to cheer his arrival.

Lindbergh's feat brought back to me a vivid memory of my own "exploit" three years earlier. Commercial flying was in its precarious infancy when I took a plane—an old biplane crate—from Paris across the English Channel to London. Only a few brave souls had done it. A relative traveling with me thought I was nuts. He took the boat-train and met me in London. My flight was a three-hour stomach-churning affair. After we landed, it took me three days to recover. I knew not what I was doing.

But Lindbergh knew what he was doing. His was a fantastic adventure, flying alone from Long Island 3,000 miles across the ocean in this little one-engine plane without any of the modern protections.

The odds looked bad when he took off all by himself. Others had made earlier unsuccessful efforts. But Lindbergh made it.

The French were a little unhappy that an American rather than a Frenchman had flown across the Atlantic. But they had to admit it was sensational.

On that day, Lindbergh instantly became the most famous person in the world. Then he spent the rest of his life proving what a relatively low-class fellow he was otherwise. He became a pal of Adolph Hitler's. He thought Hitler was a genius.

Before Lindbergh's flight, I was spending my days engrossed in art, paying little attention to the scientific and political worlds. But Lindbergh's attainment created a contagious excitement, a feeling that one individual could do anything. The world was opening up.

Art and literature were flourishing. Now Lindbergh had proved that voyages of the mind and the imagination could be made real.

FROM BRIDGEPORT TO PARIS

I got to Paris via Bridgeport, Connecticut, and New York City. I was born in Bridgeport on July 21, 1903, the youngest of three children. My father was a businessman. My mother, a native of Chicago, was an accomplished pianist.

We moved to New York City when I was six to give my mother greater access to the concerts and operas she loved and to provide a broader cultural and social life for my sister, brother, and me. We had been in New York only about three years when my mother died. Four years later, when I was twelve, my father died. My safety net was the love of my remarkable sister Ruth, with whom I lived in Manhattan near Columbia University.

I was twenty years old when I read John Galsworthy's popular novel, *The Forsyte Saga*. Among other virtues, it described the practice of well-to-do English families sending their children to the continent to broaden their education.

Unlike the Galsworthy characters, I had no parents to send me abroad. After one semester at New York University, I quit college and went to work in the home decorating department of B. Altman & Company, a fine department store in its day. A coworker, Anne Washington, reputed to be a direct descendant of George, told me that I had aesthetic talent. I was just seventeen when she said that, and I have never forgotten it, nor the kindness of Anne and her friends. They took me to concerts and art galleries and encouraged me to study painting. In less than six months, I decided that I would never be a really good painter. Instead, I became a passionate art lover.

I had a $30,000 inheritance from my father that provided an income of about $2,000 a year, almost enough to live on in that long ago time. Under the spell of the Galsworthy novel, I decided to use my income to send myself to Paris.

It was a terrific decision. The years I lived in Paris, from 1924 to 1929, were my substitute for a college education and my training ground for a future as an art collector.

In the summer of 1924, I sent myself to France in style, sailing first class on a French liner, meeting fascinating people and eating obscene quantities of caviar. The magnificent meals continued on the boat train from Cherbourg to Paris as I gazed out at the beautiful French countryside.

I moved into a Parisian hotel room on the Right Bank, on the Rue de Rivoli, just a short walk to a feast for my eyes that would profoundly influence my life—the Louvre.

LOVING THE LOUVRE

On my first day in Paris, I went straight to the Louvre. I continued to go at least three times a week. It was not nearly as crowded as it is today, so it was possible to see masterpieces without security barriers.

Instead of entering through today's glass pyramid, you walked directly up the Daru staircase. I was overwhelmed, as were millions before me, by the enormous Hellenistic *Winged Victory of Samothrace*. The eight-foot marble goddess of victory, an idealized female body with huge wings, was created for the prow of a battle ship. It literally took my breath away. The sculpture signified everything: the power, the ship, and the earth traveling through the universe. We will never know the name of the artist who carved this masterpiece.

In the Egyptian section, I was captivated by a small wooden sculpture called *The Scribe*. That intriguing little piece made a big impression on me, spurring my interest in ancient art. My reaction to *The Scribe* was almost reverential. I was an extremely idealistic young man with a bit of an inferiority complex. I felt I had to learn all the time because I knew so little. To me, *The Scribe* represented great knowledge. Revering it somehow gave me confidence in my own judgment, which helped me in my personal life and in the art world.

After being so moved by *Winged Victory* and *The Scribe*, I found myself less impressed by the Louvre's large roomful of Rubens. We now know that some of them were really painted by his atelier. Of course, several famous artists had virtual factories.

None of the great artists in the Louvre—not even Michelangelo or da Vinci (notwithstanding my fascination with the *Mona Lisa*)—had the same impact on me as the anonymous sculptures I saw on my first day in Paris: *Winged Victory* and *The Scribe*.

But I found, returning again and again to the Louvre, that certain paintings were increasingly interesting. This was an early lesson in self-education. Each time you return to a work of art, you observe different things about the composition, the draftmanship, the placement of figures and objects, the relationship between colors. It is the confluence of all of these elements, and many others, that evokes an emotional response.

Anyone who has seen my collection, or at least a substantial part of it, knows that I love color. It was Matisse's marvelous colors that attracted me to his paintings in Paris. I had the same response when I first saw Milton Avery's work. I think Jackson Pollock's *Number 8*, which hangs in the Neuberger Museum, uses color better than many of his other paintings. People who love Mark Rothko certainly respond to his sense of color, which is evident in his *Old Gold Over White*, another purchase that I gave to the Neuberger.

Sometimes it is a passionately strong use of color that attracts me, or sometimes it is a romantic subtlety, as in the various shades of green used by Georgia O'Keeffe in her haunting landscape, *Lake George by Early Moonrise*, evocative of Matisse's use of various shades of one color.

One principle is as true today as it was when I first entered the Louvre: Whether you are studying the composition, the color, or any other aspect, you never tire of looking at a masterpiece. You can go back to it countless times and each time see something new. This is the excitement of loving art.

SETTLING INTO PARIS

It was my good fortune to run into a man who had spent several years in Paris under assignment from R. H. Macy. They were training him to be a merchandiser and he was on his way home, giving up his room and selling his Citroen convertible, which I bought for $400. I also took over his room in a large house with an attached garage on a little street called Rue Nicholas about a half-mile from the Bois de Boulogne in the Passy section of Paris. I think the number of the house was 36.

In the house were a French school teacher, his wife, their little boy, and me, the new tenant, who seized this great opportunity to accelerate my fluency with a French family. A frequent visitor contributed to my extra-curricular education—the school teacher's thirty-year-old sister, who lived in a province outside Paris. She came to the city ostensibly to shop, perhaps a Madame Bovary type, a little bored with her country husband, but apparently not with me. I sometimes felt like a character in a Colette novel.

Many years later, in 1984, I was standing on line outside the Louvre with my wife Marie and our daughter Ann on our last day in Paris. Impulsively, I said, "Goodbye, girls, I am going to see the city on foot." I took a long walk, strolled up the Champs Elysee, turned left, and found Rue Nicholas. The house had been replaced by a six-story apartment building. My memories remained.

As a young man, it had been hard to leave that comfortable house, with its many amenities, but I really wanted to be on the Left Bank where the artists were. I found a large, airy apartment in the heart of the Left Bank, at 119 Boulevard St. Germain.

The apartment was a four-minute walk to the Café des Deux Magots, where I joined a group of young people who gathered nearly every day. We sat for hours and talked about ideas and art, as young people had done at that café for more than a century.

But though I had friends and a romance or two, I did not have nearly the same pace of social life in Paris as I had in New York. The flood of Americans in Paris included very few Jews who were reading and studying art as I was.

My roommate on Boulevard St. Germain was Herman Wechsler, whom I had met in a French course at the Berlitz school. Herman was on a two-year scholarship from New York University to study art in Europe. We shared several apartments over the years, and we became close friends. He, too, was an avid reader. Together, we took a course in book binding. I didn't think I had any particular facility for it, but I found to my amazement that I became pretty good at it. I enjoyed it, particularly when I could bind Aldous Huxley and other favorite writers. I still have some books I bound more than seventy years ago.

Herman and I often walked from our apartment to the Café des Deux Magots, where, like most of the customers, we drank moderately, often a creme au chocolat or something called export cassis, not a very intoxicating drink.

Only a few expatriates like Hemingway drank heavily of pernod and red wine.

One July evening in 1926, I entered the Café des Deux Magots and noticed a young man under verbal assault by some pseudo-intellectuals who were baiting him. He was obviously a brilliant student with a remarkable mind.

His name was Meyer Schapiro, he was twenty-one years old, a year younger than I was, and he had already earned a Bachelor of Arts degree with honors in art history and a Master of Arts degree from Columbia. He would later become a MacArthur Fellow and a University Professor at Columbia.

In this architectural debate at the café, Meyer's adversaries were trying to trip him up in a discussion of the flying buttress. Meyer said that this motif, revealed in the artistic rendering of a horse with its legs extended out both in front and in back, impossible in reality, first appeared in two works a thousand miles apart. The two artists could not possibly have known each other, or been familiar with each other's work. This kind of coincidence has occurred many times in history. Often a breakthrough invention takes place in one part of the world and a similar invention occurs in another part of the world. So it was with the flying buttress.

Meyer Schapiro was a vigorous, extremely knowledgeable speaker, a fanatical salesman of ideas, and a pretty good painter as well. He came out fine in the debate and we became instant friends.

Shortly after this incident, Meyer left Paris for a long trip through Europe. He returned in October, when most American tourists had gone home. Herman Wechsler was in America visiting his parents so there was room for Meyer to stay at my Left Bank apartment. After working hard on scholarly projects, studying Romanesque art during his travels, he was ready to relax and enjoy the sights of Paris. Later, he returned to New York to complete his doctoral studies in art history at Columbia.

Meyer Schapiro, who died in 1996, became the preeminent twentieth-century art historian and teacher of art history. I was an early and lucky beneficiary. His students at Columbia were astounded by his eloquence and teaching ability. He often came to dinner at my home in New York. I was never more pleased than when Meyer would put his stamp of approval on a new work of art in my collection.

I always felt that Herman Wechsler also had the potential to be an important scholar, in the Meyer Schapiro mode. But he did live a lively life and was fun to be with. He had a flair.

He became quite successful in the arts, writing books on prints and becoming one of the first to open a gallery on Madison Avenue, the F A R Gallery (Fine Art Reproductions), a beautiful place. I thought he made a mistake by dealing in reproductions rather than originals. But Herman reasoned that because of the depression, it was better to deal in less expensive pictures. If he had dealt in originals, he might have been an outstanding dealer.

He also had a business on the far East Side of Manhattan where he framed paintings beautifully, including some in my collection. He framed Milton Avery's *Gaspé Landscape*, which I brought to him directly after I purchased it in January 1943.

Herman died in 1976. In May 2002, his sister and brother-in-law established the Herman J. Wechsler Award at New York University for study and travel on the continent. When he was my roommate in Paris, Herman didn't have the money to study abroad. His scholarship from New York University may well have changed his life. The Wechsler Award is a wonderful way to honor his memory.

In late fall of 1926, with both Herman and Meyer gone home to America, I left damp and chilly Paris for the south of France and spent three months on the tennis circuit. In Cannes, I managed to beat the great Fred Perry, who was then sixteen years old. But I was having too much fun. I developed a guilty conscience enjoying myself so fully and not doing a lick of work.

I returned to Paris and, using my experience at B. Altman, went to work for Alexandre Dumas, a Parisian decorating firm in the avant garde of modern wallpaper and other art deco decor. They also had a basement full of antiques. My job paid $10 a week plus 10 percent commission on sales. At a fortuitous time in the fluctuations of the franc, I sold $50,000 worth of antiques. With my commission from that sale, I could afford to spend all of my time immersed in art, haunting the museums, reading, drinking coffee and wine at the cafés, living the life of a Left Bank student.

I watched street artists at work, visited galleries, studied the Impressionists at the Luxembourg, went to the Louvre and enrolled at the Sorbonne in an eye-opening course taught by Walter Pach, a

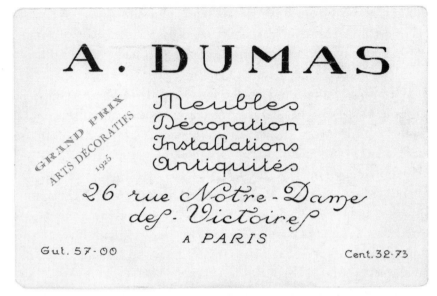

Roy's business card for A. Dumas, the decorating firm where he worked in Paris.

good artist, a distinguished scholar, a major writer and educator. Under his tutelage, I first began to think about collecting.

Pach was brilliant, articulate, adventurous, inspirational, everything a teacher should be. At that time he was in his thirties, already on his way to becoming a legendary figure. He was one of the illustrious group of sponsors of the 1913 Armory Show in New York, which introduced European Modernism to America.

Walter Pach was a man of superb taste. Some years ago, reading the provenance on the back of a picture in my collection, I discovered that I had bought a painting he once gave to his wife. It is a small painting by Morton Schamberg, *Machine Forms*, which I regard as a masterpiece, a Vermeer of the twentieth century.

The Schamberg is one of the earliest pictures depicting industrial America. Although it is small—just 6¾ inches by 5 inches—it was once valued at $250,000. I loaned it to a number of shows, including one at the British Consulate in New York. Now it is at the Neuberger Museum of Art.

THE PARIS SCENE

The leading American expatriates in Paris were literary figures older than me—Gertrude Stein, Ernest Hemingway, Scott Fitzgerald, and their friends. The writer I knew best was Thornton Wilder, a fascinating conversationalist. He had just published *The Bridge of San Luis Rey*, which won the Pulitzer Prize. Wilder was a man with a real wanderlust. He could not stay in one place for more than a week or two. He would come and go to Paris, Vienna, and all the great European capitals.

Expatriate painters were not as well known as the writers, even though many of our best artists went to Paris to study. American painters, including James Whistler, John Singer Sargent, Thomas Eakins, and Maurice Prendergast, had been working in Paris before the turn of the century. Prendergast made the last of several trips to France and Italy in April 1914, just before the start of World War I.

The so-called "Great War" was a convulsive and shattering experience for Europe. More people were killed than in any other war in history. The slaughter of French, English, and German youth was staggering. We were affected, but less so. America entered the war after much of the carnage had taken place. Soon after the armistice, Americans began pouring into Europe, eager to see the homelands of parents and grandparents, but coming to know European countries from quite a different perspective.

After the misery of World War I, Paris in the 1920s was a unique time and place for the pleasures of life. You got the euphoric feeling that war was a thing of the past.

Some of the young Americans, like me, were there primarily for the art scene. When I arrived in Paris, Picasso was already a revered old master, as was Braque. I liked their work, though I preferred Matisse, and still do. I'm not saying that Matisse is a greater artist than Picasso, but if I had to choose between a major Matisse or a major Picasso, I would choose the Matisse. Visually his work gives me more pleasure.

Showing Matisse and Picasso in the same exhibition is an inspired idea. Such a show opened at the Tate Modern in London in May 2002, and is traveling widely. Putting the work of these two artists side by side underscores their brilliance and their differences. Picasso's more experimental work is often presented in muted colors—tan, gray, and brown. Matisse took fewer chances than Picasso in composition, but his work is an exuberant explosion of color. I'm told that Picasso said, "Matisse's use of color is uncanny." And, he might have added, uncannily moving.

One of my favorite shows was Matisse in Morocco, which I came upon some years ago in Washington, before it came to New York. It was a relatively small show and an exciting discovery.

I also prefer Vermeer to Rembrandt. Rembrandt and Vermeer are both giants, but there are a ton of Rembrandts in the world and only a handful of Vermeers.

In my first days in Paris, I fell in love with Seurat, van Gogh, and Cezanne. To me, those are still the Big Three. Seurat's *Sunday on La Grande Jatte-1884*, now in the Art Institute of Chicago, is a collection in itself. I went twice to the Stephen Sondheim musical based on Seurat, *Sunday in the Park with George*, even though I knew that it presented a sanitized view of France in the 1880s. So does much of the painting from that time. Artists show the French as better than they were.

When I arrived in Paris, the Impressionists and Post-Impressionists were long gone. Manet had died in 1883, van Gogh took his own life in 1890. Seurat, who lived only to the age of thirty-one, died in 1891. Cezanne, barely made it into the twentieth century. He died in 1906. They were just beginning to be recognized as great artists, but other modern artists were alive and flourishing. I enjoyed the works of Fernand Leger and Fujita, who I thought was a very good draftsman, if not a really great painter. Fujita was extremely popular at that time in Paris, more so than Picasso. He was painting European rather than Asian pictures.

Utrillo, who painted almost exclusively Parisian street scenes, was all the rage. He painted beautifully from 1909 to 1911 and then spent the rest of his life copying himself. Today, Utrillos are sold for millions of dollars. Personally, I think people are throwing their money away. Many of the Utrillos that command such prices look to me like reproductions. I felt that way even in 1925, when I saw Utrillo shows in Paris.

Looking at art, absorbing it visually, is the most important part of an education in art. But I also believe in reading. Early on, I read four volumes by the astute art critic Bernard Berenson, in which he explains tactile values—what you touch and feel. I became aware of developing my own tactile reactions to paintings.

Another of my early educators was the writer George Moore. Very few people have heard of Moore. You had to be in Paris in the 1920s to know about him. He was an aristocrat and also a painter who wrote *Confessions of a Young Man*. He wasn't a major artist, but he provided a useful education about the modernists, recounting how people laughed at them when they first came on the scene.

Moore wrote about "the natural man, who educates himself, who allows his mind to grow and ripen under the sun and the wind of modern life, in contra-distinction to the University man, who is fed upon the dust of ages . . ." This had strong appeal to my natural tendency toward academic truancy.

Meyer Schapiro urged me to read a recently published book by James Joyce called *Ulysses*. I still have the volume, nicely bound, that I read in 1926, shortly after Shakespeare and Company published it in Paris. Few Americans were familiar with this book because it had been banned in the United States. I didn't understand *Ulysses* at first, but it gradually reached me. I never forgot Joyce's description of a beach as the vastness of eternity.

The book that exerted the strongest emotional impact on me during my Paris years was *Vincent van Gogh* by Floret Fels, edited by Henri Floury, and published in Paris in 1928, the year I read it. My copy still occupies a prominent place on my bookshelf. The printed pages are now yellowed and crumbling, held together by a rubber band.

Today, the story of van Gogh's sad and impoverished life is well known. In 1928, I was appalled to learn how unappreciated he had been. For six years, from 1885 to 1890, he lived in his beloved south of France and painted glorious pictures, his greatest works.

He painted *The Potato Eaters* in 1885 at the age of thirty-two. If he had died then, he never would have become famous because *The Potato Eaters*, to my eyes, is a mediocre painting compared to the wonderful paintings he produced in subsequent years.

France is a country that loves art, but no one bought any of his paintings, despite valiant efforts by his brother Theo to sell them. Finally, in despair, van Gogh killed himself.

I concluded that the French had a great opportunity and flunked. But I also learned a broader lesson from the book: that the contemporary world is too often uninterested in the contemporary artist. France's miserable treatment of van Gogh was an experience shared by artists in nearly every period and country. I didn't want twentieth-century America to flunk the way the French had in the nineteenth century. I decided to do what I could to prevent a recurrence of the van Gogh story. I would help support living artists, buying their works and championing their causes. I would collect living artists myself, and urge museums and other collectors to do likewise.

To accomplish this, I would need capital. So in 1929, at the age of twenty-five, I left Paris and went to Wall Street, an arena I knew absolutely nothing about, but where I was determined to make my fortune.

THE LAST TIME I SAW PARIS

Young people flocked to Paris in the 1920s to study visual arts, just as they went to Vienna for music and medicine. Paris was perfect for me when I lived there. I loved the art, the food, the excitement of the city, and the clash of ideas in the cafés.

The last time I saw Paris was in 1984, on a trip celebrating my daughter's fiftieth birthday. We stayed near the Louvre, at the same hotel on Rue de Rivoli where I lived after my arrival in 1924. I still love Paris. Architecturally, it is the most beautiful city in the world. But I doubt I will go there again. At ninety-nine, I want the comforts I have at home in New York. As a place to live, New York is now the center of the world.

The Neubergers, the Averys, and friends poolside at Florival Farm, the Neuberger country home, late 1950s. (Left to right) Peggy Freydberg, Nicholas Freydberg, Milton Avery, Sally Avery, Marie Neuberger, and Roy Neuberger. (Photo by Connie Kanaga.)

CHAPTER TWO

A COLLECTION BEGINS

When my ship docked in New York in March 1929, Wall Street was ablaze with prosperity. After five years abroad, I was fired by enthusiasm for art. But to become a collector, I had to earn money. Wall Street was the place to go.

I began as a runner, sort of a glorified messenger, and was soon promoted to the brokerage training program. When the October Panic occurred—the great stock market crash on Black Tuesday, October 29, 1929—I was a young man of twenty-six just two months into a new job.

The only stocks I managed during the Panic were my own. The glamour stock in 1929 was Radio Corporation of America (RCA), much overpriced in my view, so I went short on it. When the Panic occurred, I had enough profit from going short on RCA to offset losses on other stocks. Many others, older and wiser than me, were not so lucky.

Wall Street turned out to be a serendipitous choice. Although I went there to make enough money to buy art, it was soon clear that I had some talent for the activities on Wall Street. Its romance and excitement captivated me. It became the second passion of my life.

My job on Wall Street was fortunate for yet another reason. One day, while studying a stock in the research department, I spotted a pretty young researcher with a great figure, Marie Salant, who would later become my wife.

DUNCAN PHILLIPS AND THE PHILLIPS COLLECTION

Shortly after the October Panic, over Thanksgiving weekend, 1929, I was visiting a friend in Washington and made a discovery that affected the rest of my life. I went for the first time to the Phillips Gallery and asked to meet Duncan Phillips, an elegant man seventeen years my senior.

The Phillips Gallery was the first museum to highlight living American artists. On my first visit, I was overwhelmed by the mix of contemporary Americans with the Post-Impressionists who had excited me in Paris. I liked everything I saw, even Renoir, who is usually not one of my favorites. But Renoir's *The Luncheon of the Boating Party* at the Phillips Gallery is full of vibrant colors and bursting with energy. To my mind, it is a great picture. The Phillips Gallery showed just enough historical art to demonstrate the influences of the past and the transitions that occur in style and taste. I saw paintings there by El Greco and Delacroix and Daumier. The Phillips showed a quite different sort of Daumier than is usually exhibited.

The Uprising, a large oil painted in about 1860, depicts a militant group marching through Paris. The gallery also exhibited several powerful smaller Daumiers.

I told Duncan Phillips how much I enjoyed his collection, and that I too had lived in Paris and was an art lover who wanted to collect the work of living artists. Although he was quite shy, he was friendly and helpful. From the moment I met him, he was my artistic mentor, the collector I looked up to more than any other. He was in his prime, forty-three years old, when I was a young man of twenty-six. I developed enormous respect for him and was always interested to see what he was buying. I watched his collection grow, studied the artists he bought and learned from his choices. Phillips liked many artists whose work appealed to me.

Duncan Phillips mixed El Grecos and Renoirs with modern artists like Stuart Davis, Arthur Dove, Joseph Stella, Edward Hopper, John Marin, Marisol, and Georgia O'Keeffe. It was a big break for an artist to have Phillips as a patron.

I was proud that in 1955 the Phillips Gallery mounted an exhibit of fifty paintings from my collection.

The weekend at the Phillips Gallery strengthened my determination to collect art. But a few other things kept me busy.

Marie Salant and I were married in 1932 in the depth of the depression, on a day when the Dow Jones had sunk to 42. Two years later, our daughter Ann was born, later joined by Roy and Jimmy. I was building a family and a career. At the same time, my taste in art, hardly audacious, was developing.

WHY I BOUGHT WHAT I BOUGHT

I loved the sense of exhilaration and discovery I felt when looking at great art. A trip to a museum could make my spirits soar. I can still feel today the elation I felt on my first visit to the Phillips Gallery, enhanced enormously by meeting Duncan Phillips.

When I was buying, I often went to a museum to see masterpieces before going out to a gallery to look at a painting or a piece of sculpture that I might buy. I might go to a Degas show, perhaps for only a half-hour. I would then go out and look at unknown works. It was a good test, a good thing to do. I think it was excellent training.

It was also a great help to me that I am a gregarious character. It was easy for me to become friendly with gallery owners and museum people.

Some collectors have people shopping for them. The Morgans and Rockefellers had Lord Duveen buy their art. Joe Hirshhorn, whose collection is at the Hirshhorn Museum in Washington, had a man who bought for him.

For better or worse, I never did that. I made my own selections, lived with my own decisions. My guides were my own looking at many pieces of art, reading, and talking to everyone. I loved to listen to people talking about art. As I became more confident in my judgment, I began to talk about art myself.

Perhaps my most influential guide was intuition. Only in retrospect do I recognize what attracted me to certain pictures:

1. A high degree of creativity as expressed in composition, form, technique, and relation to space.
2. What was the artist up to? Trying to say? Trying to do? Often the communication was: "I love these colors and these textures." Certainly, that was key with Jackson Pollock.
3. An affinity for European painting, rooted in my early years in Paris. It was a French quality that initially attracted me to Milton Avery and Max Weber.
4. Color. I love the skillful use of color.
5. Humor. Not always but sometimes. That was one reason that Alexander Calder appealed to me.

6. Figures—striking ones. Although my collection includes some terrific Abstract Expressionist art, I like compelling figures.

EARLY ACQUISITIONS: GROPPER, MACCOY, AND HURD

I began buying a little, very cautiously. In 1937, I bought a small paper and ink drawing, *Two Men Pouring Wine*, by William Gropper, a socially conscious painter as prominent for his political activities as for his art. But there is nothing overtly political about this painting. The men could be union organizers or laborers on a break. The lines are simple and vivid. I bought the Gropper, an inexpensive piece suitable for a young man with a young family, and some other paintings by left-wing artists, from the A.C.A. Gallery, still in existence today and still a very good gallery.

That same year the Metropolitan Museum bought a Gropper oil painting that was severely criticized by conservative critics. Today, Gropper seems tame, but during the depression years of the 1930s he was a highly controversial artist.

Also in 1937, Marie and I bought Guy Maccoy's *February Feeding*, a winter farm scene. Maccoy was from a small town in Kansas, so this was a natural subject for him. The painting was not a bad choice for a beginner. Maccoy has since been collected by the Metropolitan and other museums, although he is not as important a figure in history as Gropper.

Maccoy was attempting to bring together three art trends: Regionalism, Precisionism, and Surrealism. It was an impossible task, but I still regard *February Feeding* with some affection.

In 1939, I made my first moderately important purchase, *Boy from the Plains*, by Peter Hurd, a portrait of a sun-baked eighteen-year-old farm boy. Peter Hurd was a handsome guy, an excellent Realist, married to Andrew Wyeth's sister Henrietta. Like Wyeth, he painted interesting portraits against the American landscape. Hurd and Wyeth were both students of Wyeth's father, the artist N. C. Wyeth.

Why do you buy one painting and pass up another? Perhaps, in this case, the painting evoked the Italian Renaissance, a period I love. It reminded me of a fifteenth-century Italian portrait. The picture is a straightforward, direct, simple composition (though not crude) and very appealing.

Nelson Rockefeller shared my admiration for *Boy from the Plains*. Shortly after I acquired it, Nelson borrowed it for an exhibition of American art which President Franklin D. Roosevelt sent to South America as part of his "Good Neighbor" policy.

I bought another Peter Hurd a year or so later, a larger painting called *The Rainy Season*, which is one of four paintings, including Milton Avery's *Sunset* that I gave to the Brooklyn Museum in 1945.

Like his paintings, Peter Hurd was a straightforward person. He was chosen to paint the official portrait of President Lyndon B. Johnson. When it was finished, President Johnson said it was the ugliest thing he had ever seen. It is now in the National Portrait Gallery in Washington, with other presidential portraits. Some people think the painting flatters Johnson.

I purchased the Peter Hurd from Mary Sullivan, whose husband Cornelius, a wealthy lawyer, lost his money in the 1929 crash. Mary Sullivan was forced to change from collecting art to running a gallery. She was encouraged by Arthur Davies, an artist who was a key organizer of the historic 1913 Armory show in New York of modern art. In my opinion, Davies was not really a great artist (though I admire his 1880 painting, *Romance*, which is in my collection) but he had an important influence on the development of twentieth-century art. Mary Sullivan was a former art teacher and one of the women, all serious collectors with strong opinions, who founded the Museum of Modern Art.

BUYING ARTISTS EARLY

As I built my collection, I was acquiring what I felt intuitively were fine works by young artists.

It happened that most of the paintings were freshly created by artists still in an early stage of their careers, the point at which they would need recognition, help, and encouragement.

Jacob Lawrence and Jack Levine, for instance, were in their twenties, Peter Hurd and William Baziotes were in their early thirties, and scores of others were early-career artists I included in my collection, most with works they had created within a year or so, sometimes within months, of my purchase.

This approach, I was told, made me an uncommon collector. I was told also that other collectors were watching carefully what I was buying. Some felt I was prescient.

Actually, I was not interested in art as an investment, although collecting the work of young, relatively unknown artists did carry with it a sense of adventure and the need for quick decisions similar to the lure of Wall Street.

Most of the works I bought were not yet acceptable to the public at large. People were still focused on the great art of the past or on European contemporary art.

SAMUEL KOOTZ, STUART DAVIS, AND WILLIAM BAZIOTES

I met Sam Kootz in 1942 when he was an unemployed advertising man whose business had gone to pieces during the first year of World War II. Some people are land poor or house poor: They have a lot of land or a big house but not enough money to pay the bills. Sam was "art poor." His walls were covered with modern paintings. He had nothing else.

A friend urged me to help Sam by buying a painting from him. I went to his home and bought the Stuart Davis *Barber Shop*, which I have come to love and to feel is a work of major importance. It was a daring purchase at the time that I made it, a Cubist-inspired semi-abstraction. Ten years later, Alfred Barr, director of the Museum of Modern Art, tried to buy it from me for MoMA. By then, it had become one of my favorite paintings.

I rate Stuart Davis as one of twentieth-century America's most important artists, along with Edward Hopper, David Smith, Milton Avery, and Alexander Calder. There is something very strong and succinct about this painting. Its bright colors show the momentum of New York City against a background of a simplified Brooklyn Bridge. By 1942, I understood enough about art to believe I had some judgment of what was great. I believed this was a great painting.

More than 95 percent of my purchases were from galleries, where most artists sell their work. At that time, the usual financial arrangement was two-thirds of the price to the artist and one-third to the gallery, which covered the cost of running the gallery and mounting and advertising the show. For most of my purchases, I was assured that the artist would be the major beneficiary.

The one exception, which I still feel badly about six decades later, was Stuart Davis. The dynamic *Barber Shop* was owned outright by Sam Kootz. Nothing from that purchase went to Davis. Later I bought Davis' *Shapes of Landscape Space 1939* from Edith Halpert of the Downtown Gallery, where it had been placed on consignment by its owner, Mrs. Irvine Shubert of the theatrical family. The purchase price was divided between the gallery and Mrs. Shubert. Davis got nothing from either of my purchases.

During his lifetime, Davis was pretty much ignored. He was so short of money that he paid his doctor with paintings which the doctor really didn't understand or care for. Eventually, Davis was successful, but it came quite late in his life, as it does with many artists. Even Alexander Calder, who is highly regarded today and had a tremendously popular show at the East Wing of the Smithsonian in Washington in 1998, didn't attain real success until the 1950s, when he was in his late sixties.

At the end of World War II, Sam Kootz opened a gallery on Madison Avenue. Today, Madison Avenue is famous the world over as the site of highly respected galleries. Sam was a pioneer on Madison Avenue and I was his first customer. On opening day, I bought a William Baziotes, my first acquisition of an Abstract Expressionist painting, an untitled picture clearly the work of a subtle and sensitive painter unknown to the public, like most Abstract Expressionists. Five years later, I acquired Baziotes' *Dying Bird*, a strong, haunting painting, bought within months after it was created.

At Sam's apartment near the Metropolitan Museum, Marie and I, one night at dinner, met William Baziotes and his wife. Baziotes was a modest fellow, highly regarded as an Abstract Expressionist, though he has his own whimsy. A really good artist has his own signature style. You can tell by looking at a painting that it is a Baziotes and not, for instance, a Stamos, another fine artist of Greek descent. I didn't buy a Stamos and he never forgave me. I probably made a mistake. I think Stamos is quite good.

MILTON AVERY: AN AMERICAN ORIGINAL

My collection is often associated with the extraordinary American painter Milton Avery not only because I have owned more than 100 Averys but also because I am so enthusiastic about him.

Early in his career, Milton Avery was recognized by some art critics and fellow artists as a man of exceptional talent, but the public was slower to recognize his genius. His reputation has grown steadily. Now, in the early twenty-first century, he has become hugely popular with the wide audience his work merits. I am proud that I recognized his talent early and bought many of his finest works.

One distinguished critic, Clement Greenberg, who initially dismissed Milton as a lightweight, later recanted and said that Milton had created "some of the most unmistakably and authentically American art that I, for one, have seen."

I have never wavered in my original opinion. Avery, to my mind, was an American Matisse. Although he did not visit France until 1952, at age sixty-seven, his work always showed a French touch, the kind of sensibility that attracted me to French painting when I lived in Paris.

Like Matisse, he was a color magician, using simplified planes of color, though, in keeping with his New England background, Milton's colors tended to be more sober.

He has been compared not only to Matisse, but also to Turner, Bonnard, Monet, and Cezanne.

Artists have been influenced by those who came before them since the era of cave paintings. Many artists have affected the styles of Raphael or of Michelangelo, perhaps the greatest artist who ever lived. There is no question that Avery was familiar with the works of earlier artists, including Matisse, but he was clearly his own person, an American original.

There is something very American, a rugged, robust feeling, in much of his work, although Milton was a very gentle person. This quality shows particularly in the strong *Self Portrait (1941)*, which I am crazy about and move from room to room in my home.

Milton's work, though seemingly simple in approach, shows a masterful sense of composition and a color sense so unbelievably elegant that it gives me intense pleasure every time I look at one of his pictures.

Although I was attracted to the formal qualities in Milton's paintings, it was the excitement and emotion that most impressed me, as well as a great wit, innocence, and, above all, beauty.

Avery is a consummate artist for people who truly love paintings.

Milton Avery's *Two Figures at Desk*, 1944, oil on canvas. (© Milton Avery Trust/Artists Rights Society [ARS], New York. Photo by Oliver Baker.)

The first Avery I saw was at Valentine Dudensing's gallery, a small painting, *The Checkerboard*. I liked it immediately and wanted to buy it but apparently I didn't, because I don't have it. It was a typical Avery in its simplicity. Milton used as his subjects the ordinary things surrounding him in his daily life. He might have walked past two men playing checkers in Washington Square Park and then gone home to paint them. Sometimes he would visit a house and see something that pleased him, a chair or a vase, and that object would appear in a painting. He painted his wife and his daughter incessantly.

When I first met him, he had hardly sold anything, even though he had earned praise from such artists as Mark Rothko, Adolph Gottlieb, and Wallace Putnam. Although he was never an art teacher, Avery influenced Rothko, Gottlieb, Barnett Newman, Alex Katz, and many other artists.

My earliest direct contact with Milton Avery came about through Sam Kootz, who showed me some Avery paintings on the walls of his apartment. Like many art connoisseurs, Sam admired Milton. He viewed him as an artist of great warmth and sensitivity to color, bounding exuberance and fine simplicity, backed by good draftsmanship. Since I liked what I saw of Avery's work, Sam suggested that I call the artist directly.

On a snowy day in January 1943, I visited Milton Avery's studio, which was also his home, on the fourth floor of a walk-up building in Greenwich Village. In the crazy patchwork maze of streets in the Village, the Averys lived where West Fourth Street crosses West Eleventh Street, near Sutters, a famous French bakery.

Milton and his wife Sally were very welcoming and we had a grand time. I knew a little about his work from the few paintings I had seen, but now I saw a lot of pictures in his studio that I liked enormously. I left with a terrific painting, *Gaspé Landscape*, which Milton wrapped up to protect from the falling snow. I put it under my arm, hopped into a cab, headed straight to Herman Wechsler's framing shop, and a few days later brought the painting home.

I have given away many Averys, but the *Gaspé Landscape*, which I bought at his studio that snowy January day, still hangs in my apartment. It is to my eyes a masterpiece.

It has the delicacy of touch and freshness of color typical of Avery, combined with the sophistication that always made me feel Milton's "French sensibility." The landscape of the Gaspé peninsula is presented as an almost abstract composition, with juxtaposed blocks of color. I never tire of looking at it.

I bought *Gaspé Landscape* directly from Milton because at that moment he had no dealer. He had previously sold in bulk to Val Dudensing. About a week or two after I bought the *Gaspé*, Paul Rosenberg began representing Milton.

From my first visit to his studio, I have been a Milton Avery enthusiast. Twice, dealers with large Avery inventories wanted to retire and offered me their collections. Both times I said yes, and both times I knew every painting that I was buying.

Avery's arrangement with dealers was somewhat different from the normal two-thirds to the artist, one-third to the gallery. (Today, generally, the artist and dealer split 50–50 or sometimes the gallery takes 60 percent and the artist gets 40 percent.)

Avery sold his paintings outright to dealers, first to Valentine Dudensing and later to Paul Rosenberg, with the understanding that when the works were sold he would get an additional amount of money, perhaps 10 percent or 20 percent of the sale price. When I bought forty-six Averys from Dudensing in 1948 and fifty-two from Rosenberg in 1951, Avery received additional checks. I know of no other American artist who had such an arrangement. Avery operated more like a European artist in that respect.

In all, I acquired more than 100 Averys representing every period of Milton's production from 1930 to 1965. The only artist whose works I bought in greater quantity was Louis Elshemius, who was much admired by Milton Avery.

My visit to the Avery family was the start of a long friendship. In the summer, they often visited our home in the countryside. I recall those days as I look at a photograph in my office of Milton, Sally, and their daughter March with Marie and me near the swimming pool. Milton had a wonderful sense of humor. Sally and March were bright and lively. Sally Avery helped support the family by illustrating children's book reviews for the *New York Times* Sunday book section. In addition to being Milton's wife, she was his best friend and promoter. She believed in him and worked to help him attain the significant position in the art world that he holds today.

My friendship with Milton lasted until his death in 1965. Milton was older than Sally, who was roughly my age. When I first met them, they were poor, but they always managed to travel—to Gaspé, to Woodstock, to New Mexico. I am still in touch with their daughter, March Avery Cavanaugh, who is a fine painter in her own right. March's son is starting a career as an artist.

Often I was asked to donate Milton Averys because people knew I had a lot of them. I was glad to do it. I wanted his work to be seen all over the country. I gave Averys to institutions which later purchased more of his paintings, including the Museum of Modern Art, the Metropolitan, and the Whitney. Until my gifts, none of these museums had Averys in their permanent collections.

In 1952, the Walker Art Center in Minneapolis showed 100 works from my collection, their first exhibit ever of an outside individual collection. I went there for a week and liked the museum and the University of Minnesota. In honor of Hudson Walker, I gave the center and the University each an Avery of their choice, *Seated Blonde* and *Fantastic Rock, California*, respectively, both of them favorites of mine as well.

Adelyn Breeskin, the director of the Baltimore Museum, mounted a major exhibition to which I loaned many pictures, most of them anonymously. I let her choose an Avery for the museum to own, and she chose an excellent painting. I was also close to the people who ran the Munson-Williams-Proctor Institute in Utica, New York, and I let them choose an Avery. The Institute in Utica is an inspired building, designed by Philip Johnson.

When Pennsylvania State University and Colgate both asked me for a painting by Milton, I told them: "I'm willing to give you each a painting provided that you go to the artist's gallery and buy another one." I used this strategy many times to help other artists as well.

Giving away the Averys was helpful to Milton. People could see for themselves how good he was. Museums and colleges and individual art collectors then bought more. I have given more than sixty Averys to museums across the country, and thirty-seven to the Neuberger Museum.

I gave away hundreds of paintings—Averys and many others—but I never sold the work of a living artist. I sold stock, but I collected art.

BUILDING AN AMERICAN COLLECTION

Prior to World War II, few Americans bought modern American art. European collectors bought virtually none. The exceptions were works by a smattering of expatriates in Europe like James Whistler and John Singer Sargent.

The 1930s was a disastrous time to be an American artist. Although museums and collectors were spending hundreds of millions—perhaps billions—of dollars on art even during the depression, America was exhibiting the same attitude as the French in the nineteenth century: little enthusiasm for the native contemporary artist. In my commitment to buy the works of living artists, it often appeared that I was almost alone. It was easy for me to buy contemporary art because so few others were doing it.

Most of what I bought reflected my instinctive emotional reactions to particular works of art. But my responses were honed by years of study, beginning with the trips to museums and galleries with my coworkers at B. Altmans, then Walter Pach's classes at the Sorbonne, days spent in the museums of Paris, and a lot of reading. By the time I made my first purchases, conservative as they were, I knew a lot about art and was ready to make decisions.

Although I started cautiously, each year I bought more until by 1941 I was really freewheeling. Each year thereafter I bought at a faster and faster pace.

Few of these purchases were planned in advance. Much of the time, when I went out on a Saturday, I would say to myself: "Roy, try not to buy." Then I would see a particularly lovely work of art, and I would be smitten. My smitten self would win out over my don't-buy self.

Between 1940 and 1945, I bought the works of twenty-four artists, including Alexander Calder, Ben Shahn, Max Weber, Jacob Lawrence, Marsden Hartley, Stuart Davis, and of course, Milton Avery.

Each year I allocated a certain amount of money for art. Then in 1946, Marie and I bought our house in the country, which put a temporary halt to major collecting. That year I acquired only the semi-Cubist *Trombone Solo* by Byron Browne, which I bought from Sam Kootz.

I went back to collecting again in 1947, and in the next two years I added a dozen more artists including Lee Gatch, Adolph Gottlieb, and John Marin. Then I bought heavily in the 1950s and 1960s, adding another 170 artists, including Jackson Pollock, Joseph Stella, Larry Rivers, Louise Nevelson, and Georgia O'Keeffe; young artists of the New York School like Helen Frankenthaler, Alfred Leslie, and Morris Louis; and a number of San Franscisco figurative painters.

I also acquired a sculpture, *The Billiard Player*, an unusual work by David Smith, whom I knew well and liked a great deal.

David Smith

I have been friendly with many artists whose works I have collected. Among them has been a quartet I especially enjoyed: the painters

Milton Avery and Ben Shahn and the sculptors Sandy Calder and David Smith.

During the 1940s, I acquired only two sculptures, Calder's bronze *Snake on the Arch* and William Steig's *Nefretete*, an 8-inch-high wood and mesh sculpture, which is far more than an entertaining diversion by a famous cartoonist. One reason I confined my collecting to paintings, as I was raising my family, was that pictures can't stab small children.

In the late summer of 1950, two months before I acquired Jackson Pollock's *Number 8, 1949*, I attended a show at MoMA of the sculptor David Smith, who had created his first welded-steel sculpture in 1931.

The minute I saw *The Billiard Player* I knew that I would purchase it. Later, I was surprised to learn that it was the only sculpture David sold the entire year.

Early on, my sister bought two small sculptures from him; I remember seeing the letter from him saying he was awfully glad the check arrived.

David had done two earlier versions of *The Billiard Player*, one in 1937. When the newer sculpture was reproduced in a *Life* magazine spread, the first national attention that David received, he explained that "the billiard player has a body which merges with the table because he has to lie, lean, and become part of the table when playing." One side—the more important side—is a billiard player and the other side is a different sculpture altogether.

David Smith's work may have been influenced by Julio Gonzales, a Spanish contemporary of Picasso, who handled material somewhat similarly, though on a very small scale. David knew foundry work and materials as well as Gonzales. He had a high degree of creativity in making those materials into objects he understood. That's what sets an artist apart from the rest of us. He was also as rugged as a blacksmith, a very masculine character who worked with heavy material that required Herculean strength.

Robert Beverly Hale, the Met's curator of American art, called David's personality "pure Hemingway." Hale once said that David "believed in prowling around with the workmen. He thinks that the workmen are all God's people. And there's nothing like getting drunk and having a good bottle of red wine . . . David Smith was a highly intellectual and sensitive character, of course, yet you wouldn't know it unless you saw him and knew him for quite a little while."

I did come to know David well, and I can testify that he was indeed both tough and sensitive. He was also very bright.

In early May of 1965, shortly after David had been appointed by President Lyndon Johnson to the National Council on the Arts, I ran into him and he said, "Roy, I've got plenty of money now. You used to buy drinks, now it's my turn." He dragged me to a neighborhood café at Sixty-eighth Street and Madison Avenue. I remember thinking at the time, I haven't bought anything from David since *The Billiard Player* fifteen years ago, I must buy a second one.

That is still one of my greatest regrets. On May 23, 1965, a few weeks after we sat in that café together, David was killed in an automobile accident near Bennington, Vermont. He was fifty-nine years old.

Alexander Calder

Often, artists came to receptions at our apartment, although my wife Marie did not always share my good opinion of them. She preferred her Bryn Mawr classmates and people who, like her, were active in education and in the Ethical Culture Society.

But even Marie was captivated by one visitor: Alexander (Sandy) Calder, the most charming man in America, who had a superb sense of humor. If I had to pick one person among twentieth-century artists who was the most fun to be with, it would be Sandy Calder. I think you can tell something of his personality from *The Circus*, which is at the Whitney Museum. He made a wire, three-dimensional structure.

This "sculpture" represents a circus with many performers and has about it a great sense of whimsy.

I met Sandy in 1944 when I bought a witty, somewhat mysterious gouache on paper, an untitled piece sometimes referred to as *Male and Female*—a charming rendition of geometric shapes that evokes images of two whimsical figures. I also purchased an atypical Calder that I consider an important work, an impressive three-foot-high bronze stabile mobile, *Snake on the Arch*, created in 1944 when he was experimenting with bronze castings. I recently moved the *Snake* to a new spot in my living room, where it looks wonderful, and I am enjoying it as much as I would a new piece of sculpture. That sometimes happens when you give a piece of art a new environment.

More characteristic of the style popularly associated with Calder is *The Red Ear*, a six-foot mobile I bought in 1960, which is now in the Neuberger Museum. It is hung over a stairway and it is a big hit.

Sandy invited Marie and me to lunch at his country home in Roxbury, Connecticut, an area famous as home to artists and writers. Once I considered buying a house there. I was born in Connecticut and loved the area, but it was 100 miles away from my city apartment and office. It would have required a two-hour-plus drive every weekend.

Calder had an all-black studio, which was a bit of a shock when you first saw it, but he liked it as a neutral background for his colorful gouaches and mobile sculptures. He had all kinds of marvelous stuff in that studio.

Although Calder's gouaches are numerous, they can't compare with his work as a sculptor. I rate Calder, David Smith, and Louise Nevelson as the three best sculptors of their era in America.

Sandy wanted us to come back often to Roxbury, which was flattering. But the distance intervened, as did our involvement with Florival Farm, our country home just one hour's drive from the city. I saw Sandy frequently in New York, but I now wish I had gone more often to Roxbury.

Ogden Nash wrote a poem about what we live to regret: not the sins of commission, the things we have done, but those of omission. I agree. I have never regretted buying a painting or spending time with an artist. But there were times when I didn't buy something and later wished I had, or didn't accept an invitation and later regretted it.

One night in New York City, after a big Architectural League dinner, a group came back to our apartment at 993 Fifth Avenue, including Sandy Calder and his wife Louisa Cushing James, a great niece of Henry and William James; the art critic James Sweeney and his wife Elaine; and Edward Larrabee Barnes, the master architect of the State University of New York at Purchase. By 4 A.M., everyone had left but the Calders and the Sweeneys, who were still drinking and chatting. Marie was asleep, oblivious to the continuing party.

Calder and Sweeney were both extroverts, and Elaine Sweeney was delightful. We had a marvelous time, but I couldn't have handled a steady diet of those hours. I had to be alert to make financial decisions in my office early the next morning.

Max Weber

At the opposite end of the personality chart from Calder and Avery was Max Weber, a short, extremely bright man with an overabundance of self-confidence. He thought he was great, and he was, though I don't think that today he is as well known as Milton Avery. Marie's parents joined us once when Max Weber and his wife came to dinner. My father-in-law was fascinated by Weber's erudition and broad knowledge of the world.

Max was ten-years old when he arrived in the United States from Russia. He grew up in New York. Like me, when he was a young man in his twenties, he went to Paris. He had the great good fortune to study with Matisse.

Early in my collecting days, I knew I wanted a major Weber from his Paris period. It took me almost twenty years to find *La Parisienne*, a subtle, lyrical nude clearly demonstrating the Matisse influence, but also an example of Weber's strong personality. Even while working under Matisse, and being influenced by him, Weber was able to establish his own style.

Weber returned to New York in 1909 when he was twenty-eight years old and was one of the first Americans to introduce Modernism to the United States. Beginning in 1910, he created Cubist paintings. Art critics of the time were harsh on this new style, but Weber's fellow artists welcomed his break-through paintings. He was an intellectual inspiration to other artists.

I was quite familiar with Weber's work when, in 1945, I acquired *String Music*, a painting that I feel represents Weber at his best.

Today, Weber is well known, but he should be more widely appreciated. He was an extremely good artist.

Jack Levine

A thin young man from Boston when I met him before World War II, Jack Levine was originally a leftist painter whose pictures were quite political. I wasn't politically motivated at that time, but many people, not just left-wing artists, were worried about our social system. Levine's *The Banquet*, which I bought in 1942, shows a group of Boston politicians who are clearly up to no good. They are shown in evening clothes, dividing profits from the Boston rapid transit system fares. A dead fish on the table implies that these men, as cold as the fish, are mean and corrupt.

I met Levine about the time I bought this painting and became quite fond of him and his wife. He was a highly intelligent man who became less critical of our political system as time passed.

In 1943, while Jack was in the Army, one of his pictures was entered in a huge art competition, "Artists for Victory" run by the Metropolitan Museum of Art. People at the Met wanted to help the war effort by showing respect for contemporary artists, even though contemporary paintings and sculptures were not their primary business and the reputation of the contemporary artist wasn't always particularly good. The show seemed like a good public relations idea. The Met provided an enormous space to house over a thousand paintings and sculptures. Jack Levine won second prize and a check for $3,500, which in 1943 was like $50,000 today. It was a lot of money to a kid whose total worth at that time was probably less than $1,000.

I was in Edith Halpert's office in the Downtown Gallery when she phoned Jack with news of the prize. Jack was on KP duty in an Army camp down South, scrubbing pots and pans. When Edith conveyed the news, I heard a loud bang coming from the telephone that sounded like pots dropping to the floor.

In 1957, when I was beginning to understand the great German composer Kurt Weill and to enjoy the haunting effect of his music, I bought a large Jack Levine painting, *The Black Freighter*, which seemed to reflect Weill's music.

Modern painting and modern music had a powerful effect on each other. You could hear modern art even in the music of Rodgers, Porter, Kern, Berlin, and the Gershwins on the Broadway stage. Jackson Pollock painted while listening to music from Stravinsky to Fats Waller.

Ben Shahn

Although I liked and respected Jack Levine and thought highly of his judgment, we never had the kind of serious talks that I had with Ben Shahn and his wife Bernarda. Ben was remarkable, a little bigger and a little heavier than most people and infinitely more intellectual.

Ben became widely known for painting the story of Sacco and Vanzetti, the two Italian immigrant anarchists executed for murder. Many people felt they were innocent of any crime, but were persecuted for their political beliefs.

The first Ben Shahn painting I bought, *India*, shows four emaciated figures collapsed on the bank of the Ganges River, starving to death. It presents the complex political situation of India in a simple, dramatic way. When I bought the painting from Edith Halpert at the Downtown Gallery, she said, "Roy, you bought a picture no one else would buy because it is so unhappy."

She was right. But good art isn't just pretty pictures. Art reflects society; good and bad, pretty and not so pretty.

After *India*, I bought Shahn's *The Blind Accordion Player*, another strong painting and much better known. Some years later, Ben came across two drawings, studies for *The Blind Accordion Player*, which he sent to me as a gift. All are at the Neuberger Museum.

I enjoyed going with Ben to cafés near the Downtown Gallery on Fifty-first Street, which is not so downtown. We rarely talked about art. We talked about economics and the social factors behind economics. Sometimes after we had a few drinks, he would pump me about Wall Street. We were never drunk but our conversation was lively and uninhibited.

Shortly before he died, we went from a party at the Modern Museum to his favorite restaurant, Giordano, on Thirty-ninth Street west of Ninth Avenue, a terrific restaurant in a terrible neighborhood. He loved it. It was typical of Ben to pass up dining at a fashionable spot in favor of some obscure place with good food.

Ben was a man of good cheer and high spirits, perhaps not always sophisticated politically, but at all times an extremely sensitive and fine man.

SOME BEST KNOWN PAINTINGS

I was a relatively new collector in 1943, the owner of works by fewer than a dozen artists, when I bought *Fishermen's Last Supper* by Marsden Hartley from the great gallery owner Paul Rosenberg. Hartley's paintings were expensive—as expensive as any American paintings at that time—but I felt when I saw it that *Fishermen's Last Supper* was a work of great strength. I was confident enough as a collector by then to acquire a painting of significance by an important artist. The painting's original impact on me has remained.

Hartley's work has the simplicity of folk art combined with an abstract sense that heightens emotion. The painting's symbolism, reflecting Hartley's religious mysticism, related religion to the everyday life of a simple family of poor fishermen. It is a strong and powerful picture.

Fishermen's Last Supper, which hangs in my living room, is now among the best known works in my collection. Sadly, Hartley died just a few months after I bought the painting, at the age of seventy. Too young. He was an extremely talented painter. In 1952, I bought two more of his paintings—an exciting charcoal sketch, *The Lighthouse*, and an almost abstract oil, *Granite by the Sea, Seguin Light, Georgetown*.

In May 1998, patrons of the National Museum of American Art in Washington visited my apartment to view my collection. Several of them told me that *Fishermen* was their favorite American painting. It has been exhibited at the Whitney, the Museum of Modern Art, and in shows across the country and in Europe.

Hartley is one of the American masters from the early twentieth century in my collection, along with Arthur Dove, Maurice Prendergast, and a few others. These acquisitions, showing continuity between past and present, were inspired by my mentor Duncan Phillips' mixing of the new and the old.

Even better known than Hartley's *Fisherman* is Edward Hopper's *Barber Shop*, which I acquired in 1954. Hopper began by showing life in the small towns of America's heartland, and later captivated viewers with his evocative paintings of cities and city people.

I once called Edward Hopper a safe, conservative artist. I take it back. I'm not so sure now. I think that in *Barber Shop* he shows an abstract sense. Hopper's unmistakeable style was realistic, which went out the window with the advent of Jackson Pollock and the Abstract Expressionists. Today, realism is back. Actually, it never totally went away.

In the late 1940s, I didn't feel that I knew all about Jackson Pollock, but I recognized that he was a sincere artist, that he was using new techniques and using them effectively. He was just beginning to be recognized, and I was told that the $800 I paid in January, 1950 for his *Number 8, 1949* heated his East Hampton house for the rest of the winter. That painting, a swirl of vivid colors and shapes, and to my mind one of Pollock's best, is now at the Neuberger Museum of Art.

Jackson Pollock was a huge influence on fellow artists like Milton Resnick. I guess I must like the Resnick hanging in my office because I have kept it there for many years. It's a big painting—a bit larger than 9 feet across and 3½ feet high.

Milton Resnick has his own style. I don't care much for Resnick's later paintings. I very much like the one in my office, *Kenya*, painted in 1953.

I don't like labels. A painting is either good or it's not, it's creative or it isn't, it has a creative spirit or it doesn't. Distinctions between realism and abstraction are often meaningless. Some Renaissance art is quite abstract, and some abstract pieces communicate a sense of strength and passion, an intensity of feeling, more clearly than a realistic picture might. Great artists have always had an abstract sense. Giotto was an abstractionist. I look at Albert Bierstadt's *Gold, Grey & Brown* landscape, which I am fortunate to have purchased, and it is sheer abstraction, though it shows clear aspects of landscape.

People often ask me: Which is your favorite picture? That is impossible to answer. Some I loved when I bought them, but I don't now. Others I admire as examples of a particular trend or time. Some paintings that already have stood the test of time and I feel will still be important 100 years from now were painted by Jackson Pollock, Edward Hopper, Lyonel Feininger, Max Weber, Lee Gatch, who was also a favorite of my mentor, Duncan Phillips, and of course, Milton Avery, particularly his self-portrait.

When I began buying art in the late 1930s, I started down an ever-widening and fascinating path. I wanted to support the paintings and sculptures of artists living and working in my time, and I am proud that I have been able to help so many. I bought the work and sometimes helped their careers along; they have given me more pleasure than I could have ever hoped for.

On my fiftieth birthday—almost fifty years ago—my wife, Marie, surprised me with a birthday book containing greetings and drawings from Pollock, Shahn, Calder, Feininger, Avery, Davis, Baziotes, Marin, Hofmann, Gottlieb, Tamayo, and thirty-five other artists I am lucky to call friends. This is the book I treasure above all others.

Marie and Roy Neuberger admiring Marsden Hartley's *Fishermen's Last Supper,* which they loaned to the Whitney Museum of American Art. (Photo supplied by Smithsonian Institution.)

CHAPTER THREE

WORKING WITH THE WHITNEY

HELPING MUSEUMS ACQUIRE ART

Some art lovers donate paintings to museums. Others write checks. There is yet another way to expand a museum's collection: Give a check for the purchase of a specific painting.

The first time I did this, in 1950, was almost by accident. I got excited about a James Brooks Abstract Expressionist painting at the Peridot Gallery in Greenwich Village. Again and again I dragged my wife Marie several miles from our apartment down to the Village to see it. I loved its interplay of shapes and color. Marie was not impressed.

Looking at the painting today, I see the degree to which Jackson Pollock influenced Brooks. During the depression, they both worked for the Federal Arts Project, a branch of the WPA directed by the noted curator Holger Cahill.

An unintended benefit of this project in the pre-World War II period was that it brought young, emerging talents into contact with one another. It became an incubator for American artists who, in combination with the brilliant artists who fled the Nazis (including Andre Breton, Marc Chagall, Piet Mondrian, Jacques Lipschitz, and Max Ernst), would become preeminent in postwar America, if not the world, as the New York School.

Artists from this extraordinary group learned from each other, influenced each other, drew strength from each other's work, drank together at the Cedar Tavern in Greenwich Village and, in several instances, married each other, most notably Jackson Pollock and Lee Krasner, and Willem and Elaine de Kooning.

James Brooks would become an important member of the New York School, though I had no way of knowing this when I first saw his work—I just liked it. Hoping to change Marie's mind, I returned to the gallery with her so many times that we became friendly with the owner, Mr. Pollack, no relation to Jackson Pollock but the brother of a quite good artist, Reginald Pollack, whose abstract landscape *Labeaume Landscape III* hangs in my country house.

Marie seldom inhibited my decisions, but in this case she did. She didn't go so far as to not allow me to buy it, but it was clear that she didn't like it. I think it was too abstract for her.

The Peridot Gallery was on lower Fifth Avenue, between Washington Square Park and Eighth Street. Around the corner, at 10 West Eighth Street, was the Whitney. It wasn't really a museum then. It was an expansion of Gertrude Vanderbilt Whitney's studio.

One day after leaving the Peridot Gallery, I walked around the corner to the Whitney. My friend Lloyd Goodrich, who would become director of the Whitney, was there. Lloyd and I both served on the Board of Trustees of the American Federation of Arts. I told him that I liked the James Brooks painting but Marie didn't. I proposed a solution: I would pay for the Whitney to acquire it. Marie would not have to look at it but the public could.

Although his heart was not necessarily set on Abstract Expressionism, Lloyd said yes. I wrote one of the first outside checks—if not the first—given to the Whitney to purchase the Brooks, becoming perhaps the first Friend of the Whitney Museum. The Whitney, a museum that became very important to me, still has the Brooks painting. I bought another small James Brooks for my own collection a decade later.

Soon after my gift to the Whitney, I gave a check for a specific purchase to the greatest of all art museums, the Metropolitan. I had already purchased an exciting Hans Hofmann abstract painting, *Fruit Bowl, Version 6*, from Sam Kootz. Hofmann was a strong, vigorous, authoritarian painter, a highly influential abstract artist and widely admired teacher, but he was having trouble getting the Met to show his work. The Met's historically conservative acquisition committee was shy about venturing into twentieth-century art, particularly contemporary American art.

At that time, in the early 1950s, if I had suggested to a member of the Met committee that they buy a Hans Hofmann or a George L. K. Morris, I would have hit a brick wall. The committee might have considered both my suggestion and the artist's work audacious. But in consultation with Robert Beverly Hale, the Met's curator of American art, I arranged to give a check specifically for the Met to purchase *The Window* by Hans Hofmann, a George L. K. Morris, a Jimmy Ernst, and works of a few other living painters.

Robert Hale and I were not proposing that the Metropolitan acquire really wild paintings, however far out they might have looked to this very establishment committee. But if Hale had asked the Met to buy these pictures with its own funds, he would never have been able to acquire them.

These experiences taught me an important lesson about the inner workings of the art establishment: If a donor earmarks the money, a museum might purchase works that it never would use its own funds to buy.

ORIGINS OF THE WHITNEY

Gertrude Vanderbilt Whitney was a good sculptor, a dedicated art lover, and a great friend to artists. From the beginning of the twentieth century until her death in 1942, she purchased, exhibited, and championed the work of contemporary artists.

The purchase of contemporary art is so widely accepted today, it is difficult to realize that for much of the twentieth century hardly anyone would buy or exhibit the work of a living, breathing American artist. Museums were dedicated to history, primarily European history. Mrs. Whitney established the Whitney studio in 1914 to show her own collection. By 1929 she had more than 500 paintings and sculptures, including works by Thomas Hart Benton, Stuart Davis, Maurice Prendergast, and Edward Hopper. She offered this collection to the Metropolitan Museum, but her gift was refused. The art was too new, too modern for the Met at that time. So she set up her own museum, the Whitney Museum of American Art, which opened in 1931 in three adjoining brownstones on West Eighth Street. It was the first museum in the nation devoted exclusively to American art.

THROUGH THE YEARS: DIRECTORS OF THE WHITNEY

Juliana Force, the first director of the Whitney Museum, remained in that post until 1948, six years after the death of Mrs. Whitney. When I got to know Mrs. Force, she was already quite elderly, an impressive woman devoted to Mrs. Whitney and to the museum. She lived in an apartment above the Whitney Museum.

Once, I was on my way to a party at Juliana Force's apartment with the art critic James Johnson Sweeney and his wife Elaine. Sweeney was active with the Museum of Modern Art (he and Dorothy Miller were the first museum officials to recognize the new American painting) and for six years was the groundbreaking director of the Guggenheim Museum. He was an erudite, cultured, brilliant scholar and great fun. His wife was fun, too.

We drove down Fifth Avenue with Elaine Sweeney at the wheel of their station wagon. She was a fast and somewhat reckless driver. It was such a hair-raising trip that I have never forgotten it. I sometimes think of it today, sitting in stalled traffic on a Fifth Avenue clogged with cars. No one could get up much speed today, but that trip with the Sweeneys was a memorable roller coaster ride. It was a great relief to arrive in one piece at the calm boudoir of the quietly elegant Juliana Force, and relax in the aura of her immense artistic knowledge.

A traveling show, "Juliana Force and American Art," was created after the death of this much-loved woman, who was an important friend to artists and to a growing art-loving public. I loaned my Alexander Calder, *Snake on the Arch*, to this show, which attracted crowds at the Whitney for a month in the fall of 1949. Under the auspices of the American Federation of Arts, the show toured the country for a year.

Juliana Force's successor, Hermon More, a painter, was the director when I helped the museum acquire the James Brooks painting. More served for the decade during which the Friends of the Whitney was formed and the museum moved from Greenwich Village to West Fifty-fourth Street. The two directors who followed him were more dynamic. Both became close friends of mine.

Lloyd Goodrich was director from 1958 to 1968, a robust decade for art in America, especially in New York. During those years, I was very active with the Whitney, joining as a Trustee in 1961.

By the time another good friend, John I. H. "Jack" Baur, took the helm in 1968, I had already begun planning the Neuberger Museum and would soon resign from the Whitney Board. I had come to know and admire Jack as a curator at the Whitney and, earlier, when he was at the Brooklyn Museum.

Jack and Lloyd were gentlemen of the old school, each with some private means. Neither was terribly rich, but they had some resources. They were both gifted scholars, prolific writers, and champions of contemporary artists, though a bit conservative in their tastes. They were wonderful men with vastly different personalities. Lloyd was somewhat reserved but a warm, direct, and exceedingly nice Scotsman; Jack was a bundle of energy, outgoing, gregarious, utterly charming.

Lloyd's taste in modern art was more traditional than mine. He was a close friend of Edward Hopper and wrote an enormous book about him. He also wrote biographies of Winslow Homer, Thomas Eakins, and Max Weber. Lloyd took to the realism of Edward Hopper and Charles Burchfield more than to abstraction.

When Lloyd died in the spring of 1987, just shy of his ninetieth birthday, his son immediately contacted me as if I were one of the family. The Goodriches lived in a private house on Ninety-fourth Street near Fifth Avenue. I was there within five minutes, joining the handful of people who were close to Lloyd, including Jack Baur. Another of Lloyd's good friends, Lawrence Fleischman, a wealthy, brilliant art dealer, flew in from Detroit.

Years earlier, Jack Baur had put on an exciting show at the Brooklyn Museum spotlighting John Quidor, a long forgotten mid-nineteenth century American painter whom Jack rediscovered. Today, Quidor is a well-respected artist, somewhat like the pre-Raphaelites.

I was so captivated by Quidor's artistry that I paid a large price for three of his works at the Hirschl & Adler gallery. I gave one, *The Wall Street Gate*, to the Metropolitan Museum. Today, it is in the American Wing of the Met. The other two Quidors, a biblical scene and an outdoor tavern, are at the Neuberger Museum.

Although few people are familiar with Quidor, he is significant as a precursor of figure painters of the 1930s and 1940s and interesting in himself. He had close friendships with many writers of his time. Washington Irving inspired Quidor's painting of Ichabod Crane fleeing the headless horseman.

Jack Baur helped create the Katonah Museum near his home at Cross River in northern Westchester. It is not a collecting museum but it has become one of the most popular small museums in the country. Jack prevailed upon me to have a show there when it was located in the Katonah Village Library. In 1990, the museum moved into its own new building. People love the Katonah for its fine exhibitions and its lively social gatherings. They have a lot of fun at the Katonah.

Jack Baur retired as Whitney director in 1974 and died in 1987, less than two months after the death of Lloyd Goodrich. Ten years later, Jack's widow Louise Baur came to a League of Women Voters dinner in Manhattan at which I was honored. I was touched by this encounter, which brought back wonderful memories of warm and rewarding friendships.

Tom Armstrong succeeded Jack Baur at the Whitney and remained director for seventeen years. I liked Tom, though he may not have had the native love of art sufficient to be a great museum director. He was a terrific innovator. Under his leadership, the Whitney became the first museum to establish several corporate-funded branches in Manhattan as well as one in Stamford, Connecticut.

This development was somewhat akin to the mushrooming Guggenheim museums. The main reason little Whitneys sprang up was that the building housing the Whitney is much too small for the museum's collection. The Whitney has never had enough money. They had a tough time raising the $6 or $8 million it cost to build a new museum in 1966.

Tom Armstrong's successor, David Ross, was criticized by some as too avant garde and artistically political. Whatever controversies may have erupted, many of his exhibits were highly acclaimed. The Whitney was always a lively place during David Ross' reign in the 1990s.

In 1998, a new director with excellent credentials, Maxwell Anderson, was selected to lead the Whitney into the twenty-first century. He carries with him the good wishes of all who were present at the creation, and the enduring legacy of legendary directors who realized the dream of Gertrude Vanderbilt Whitney.

FRIENDS AND TRUSTEES

Mrs. Whitney died in 1942. In the years that followed, it became apparent that the museum needed funding beyond what could be provided by the Whitney family. Operating needs would require public support. Three of us—David Solinger, Alexander Bing, and I—set to work organizing the Friends of the Whitney Museum. By 1956, we had recruited nineteen members.

David Solinger was a lawyer, a good amateur painter, the exhusband of Hope Gimbel, daughter of the head of Saks Fifth Avenue. David was interested in the work of living artists, though he did not limit his purchases to contemporary works as I did. He also had the solid legal knowledge necessary to create the Friends and later to expand the Board of Trustees.

Alexander Bing was a member of the well-known real estate family firm Bing and Bing. He was much older than I, nearing the end of his life when I met him.

My enthusiasm for the Whitney was boundless. I gave them some pretty fine paintings and the cash to buy two Arthur Doves that are very valuable today. They were shown in the Whitney's 1998 Dove show and its 1999 review of the twentieth century.

I gave the Whitney fourteen paintings by Jacob Lawrence, comprising the series *Going Home from the War*. All fourteen were shown in the impressive Jacob Lawrence retrospective at the Whitney in

2002. It is much smaller than the famous migration series depicting African-American migration from the South to the North before and during World War II. The migration series was bought jointly by Duncan Phillips and the Museum of Modern Art, and had a tremendous impact when it was sent on tour in 1941 and 1942.

Jacob Lawrence, a key figure in the Harlem Renaissance, was a truly great artist. He painted individual pictures, but is perhaps best remembered for his series paintings.

I am crazy about the *Going Home from the War* series. There is strength and a lot of wit in Lawrence's work. All of these qualities are evident in the "Harlem" paintings he did in 1943, a narrative series that depicts every aspect of life for African Americans in New York City. My collection includes number 20 in this series of 30, "In the evening, Evangelists preach and sing on street corners."

COLLECTING FOR THE WHITNEY

Within five years, the Friends of the Whitney had enhanced the museum's collection spectacularly, broadened the fund-raising base, and attracted an enthusiastic new public to the Whitney's exhibits and educational programs.

For the first three years, I was chairman of the Acquisition Committee, and was responsible for buying a Willem de Kooning, which was considered quite an advanced picture at that time. Our committee bought a Pollock and a Hopper the same day.

We bought Alexander Calder, David Smith, James Brooks, Jose Guerrero, Helen Frankenthaler, Hans Hofmann, Franz Kline, John Marin, Robert Motherwell, Isamu Noguchi, Reginald Pollack, Abraham Rattner, Robert Rauschenberg, Theodoros Stamos, Ben Shahn, Louise Nevelson, and Charles Burchfield. Quite a list. And that is just some of what we bought. We helped the public become familiar with the work of terrific artists.

In 1961, Flora Whitney Miller, Gertrude Whitney's daughter, asked David Solinger, Lloyd Goodrich, Jack Baur, and me, to become Trustees of the museum. Until that time, the Trustees had all been members of the Whitney family.

Flora Miller had less passion for contemporary art than her mother, but as chair of the Trustees she was determined to carry on her mother's mission to broaden the audience for American artists. I liked Mrs. Miller immensely. She lived luxuriously at 10 Gracie Square, where I visited her and her husband many times, including one evening when we ate an enormous salmon caught in Canada by a Whitney relative.

Originally, David Solinger and I were the most active of the outside Trustees. Gradually, other Trustees became more active, including B. H. "Bob" Friedman, a nephew of Percy Uris. Almost all of the Trustees were conscientious about attending and participating in meetings during the eight years I served on the board.

THE WHITNEY MOVES—AND MOVES AGAIN

In 1939, the Whitney added four new galleries, nearly doubling the exhibition space of the original brownstone headquarters in Greenwich Village, but it was still too small. By 1954, Gertrude Whitney's original collection of some 500 works had grown to 1,300. The Whitney moved from Eighth Street to a new building on West Fifty-fourth Street at the rear of the Museum of Modern Art.

The opening in 1954 featured an exhibition of 100 paintings from my collection. Several times in my life, museums have opened their doors with shows from my collection. The Whitney show, mounted by Jack Baur, was the first. Others were the 1968 opening of the newest branch of the Smithsonian, the National Museum of American Art (now the Smithsonian American Art Museum), and, of course, the opening of the Neuberger Museum of Art in 1974.

Although I sometimes thought there was too much emphasis on Edward Hopper at the Whitney, I was happy that the opening show included his superb *Barber Shop*, which I had just purchased. Hopper is a master of mood, and *Barber Shop* is one of the best examples of his evocative painting. I have come to appreciate that painting more and more over the years.

The 1954 Whitney show also included paintings by Milton Avery, Arthur Dove, Jacob Lawrence, and Max Weber's 1944 painting, *String Music*. It proved to be a very popular show. Other museums asked to view the exhibit, so fifty of the paintings traveled for a year to major museums in Chicago, Los Angeles, San Francisco, St. Louis, and Cincinnati. The tour ended in 1955 in Washington at the Phillips Gallery. Other shows from my collection during the late 1950s and early 1960s were mounted in New York, Dallas, Boston, Memphis, Portland, Fort Wayne, Columbus, Ann Arbor, and elsewhere.

Attendance at the new Whitney was four times higher than at the original museum. It was soon apparent that once again public interest was outstripping the size of the facility.

The Trustees were also concerned that on West Fifty-fourth Street the Whitney was sitting in the shadow of the Museum of Modern Art. Despite the Whitney's popularity, it was difficult in that location to establish a distinctly separate identity.

Lloyd Goodrich, who was then both a trustee of the Whitney and its director, had real problems with the Modern Museum. A plan for a division of activities never really materialized. Perhaps, from the Whitney's point of view, that was just as well. What did happen did not favor the Whitney.

In the 1950s, the heads of Manhattan's three great art museums held numerous meetings to discuss the role of the Modern versus the Whitney, and the place of the Metropolitan in modern art. Francis Taylor was then director of the Met, Alfred Barr represented the Modern, and Lloyd Goodrich spoke for the Whitney.

It was agreed that the Whitney would sell its pre-1900 paintings (some of the best going to the Met) and concentrate its focus entirely on twentieth-century American art. This was not necessarily good for the Whitney because they gave up some terrific art. Taylor was very smart about this sort of thing.

A site for a new Whitney Museum was acquired in 1963 on Madison Avenue and East Seventy-fifth Street. Although it was triple the space of the West Fifty-fourth Street building, it was still too small. The Whitney collection now totaled more than 2,000 works. When the new building opened in September 1966, its first exhibition, assembled by Lloyd Goodrich from collections all across the country, attracted a crowd as large as the World Series drew the following month.

The Whitney now owns more than 12,000 works, yet the museum runs but half a block on Madison Avenue and only about 100 feet on East Seventy-fifth Street. Before it was built, you could see it would be too small. Even with a renovation in the late 1990s that created one-third more space, it is still too small.

LEAVING THE BOARD OF TRUSTEES

My departure from the Whitney Board came in 1969, precipitated by several developments. First, in June 1967, I accepted an offer from Governor Nelson Rockefeller to create the Neuberger Museum of Art on the Purchase College campus of the State University of New York. We didn't get the agreement formalized and the building erected for several years, but it was clear when I agreed to establish the museum that the major portion of my art collection would go to the Neuberger, not to the Whitney.

Then, in January 1968, I was invited to be an honorary life Trustee of the Metropolitan Museum of Art. I accepted the offer with great joy.

I began to question my role at the Whitney after the death of Edward Hopper's wife Josephine. Jo Hopper left to the Whitney a whole body of her husband's works, many of them small, but it was a large quantity—some 2,000 oils, prints, watercolors, and drawings. At the Whitney, discussions began about selling some of the paintings to raise cash. I did not like the idea of immediately thinking of these works as money, and I voiced my opinion at the board meeting quite sharply. Plans to sell were abandoned. It has never happened, that I know of.

The last straw came after I proposed that Howard Lipman, my friend and business partner, join us on the Whitney Board of Trustees. Howard was a pretty good sculptor and a generous donor to the Whitney who was keen to be an active Trustee. One of the Trustees, an important partner in Loeb Rhoades, said he didn't want to have two people from Neuberger & Berman on the Whitney Board. Without agreeing, I accepted his concerns and arranged to get off the board so that Howard could get on. Howard Lipman was later a distinguished president of the Whitney.

Perhaps the best known of the Whitney Trustees was Jackie Kennedy. While the Seventy-fifth Street building was under construction, someone suggested inviting the President's widow to join the board, and she did. They assumed that she might also give some money, but I don't think that happened. She was, of course, a charming, beautiful woman and it was good public relations to have her. She attended meetings and cut the ribbon when the East Seventy-fifth Street building was opened.

LOOKING BACK ON MY WHITNEY YEARS

In retrospect, I probably stayed active with the Whitney longer than I should have. I became pigeonholed as a collector of American art. I am a great fan of American artists, but I have broad interests in the art world.

There were many good things about my Whitney years, particularly my friendships with Jack and Lloyd and other colleagues among the Trustees and Friends of the Whitney. We accomplished a great deal and had fun along the way. I gave the Whitney a painting every year.

In later years, some of the Whitney decisions about what art to buy and to show were assailed as political. It was alleged that people who owned works by certain artists, and were anxious to have them go up in value, might use any sort of pull to have those artists shown at the museum, especially in the biennial shows.

During my years at the Whitney, that kind of thinking never entered our minds.

WHITNEY "AMERICAN CENTURY" SHOW

On Wednesday, August 18, 1999, instead of going to the office, I kept an appointment at 9:45 A.M. with Maxwell Anderson, director of the Whitney, to see the first part of the show, "The American Century Art & Culture 1900–2000." I agree with the critics who said it was the best show the Whitney ever had.

The museum was closed when I arrived. It would have been difficult for me to negotiate the long lines that formed later in the day. I was lucky. Maxwell Anderson met me at the door and went through the museum with me. The show took up the whole museum and it was marvelous.

I predict a lasting change at the Whitney, which had developed a reputation for not having great shows. This was a great show. I think Maxwell Anderson is developing into a first-rate director.

The American Century show included paintings, sculptures, photographs, and movies. A number of movies from the early days, including the classic Dashell Hammett mystery, *The Maltese Falcon*, were shown.

Art and cultural artifacts came both from the Whitney's own collection and from lenders throughout the country. Some of the art exhibited had come into the Whitney collection when I was chairman of the acquisition committee, including Alexander Calder's *Big Red*. The show also included the two Arthur Dove paintings that were acquired with money I gave the Whitney.

At one time, I disdained Grant Wood and Thomas Hart Benton. At the Whitney show, I appreciated them as really good artists—not breakthrough artists like Jackson Pollock, but each good in his own way. Seeing Grant Wood's classic *American Gothic* once again, I realized how well it describes a certain type of American.

Grant Wood was a much better painter than I thought when I first encountered him. I shouldn't have passed him up. I was familiar with the gallery that represented him and I bought other paintings from that gallery, but not Grant Wood.

The Whitney show deserved its popularity. It encouraged people to become involved in art. The curator of the show, who did a terrific job of pulling all the disparate parts together, was the critic Barbara Haskell, wife of Leon Botstein, president of Bard College.

BEING A CATALYST

Not until the mid-1970s did I realize that during my Whitney years I had become something of a catalyst for other collectors. One example is Lawrence Bloedel, who inherited a fortune from timber activities and lived in a large house in Williamstown, Massachusetts. He saw an exhibition at Williams College of fifty paintings and sculptures from my collection.

Years later, after he died, I had lunch with a relative of his who told me that I had inspired Bloedel to buy the works of modern American artists, which he did consistently and continually for the rest of his life. He left this valuable collection to the Whitney Museum.

K.H.M.'s Birthday Party (1933, oil on canvas) by Wood Gaylor, a client of Edith Halpert.

CHAPTER FOUR

THE GREAT DEALERS

A slight aura of disrespect seems to cling to the term *art dealer*, akin to wheeler-dealer, used car dealer, or a slightly unscrupulous peddler. I think it's a bad rap.

The legendary, debonair Sir Joseph Duveen, later Lord Duveen, a key player in the creation of the National Gallery in Washington, artistic advisor to John D. Rockefeller, Henry Clay Frick, and European royalty, was an art dealer. So were a renowned heiress (Peggy Guggenheim), the wife of a statesman and governor of New York

(Marie Harriman), a founder of the Museum of Modern Art (Mary Sullivan), and the son of an immortal Post-Impressionist painter (Pierre Matisse, from whom I acquired in 1947 one of my favorite paintings, Loren MacIver's famous *Portrait of Emmett Kelly*, the great clown).

Many highly respected people have became art dealers. When you change the title to "art gallery owner," a different connotation emerges.

Dealers are tremendously important in bringing artists to public attention. They not only influence what the general public buys, they also help determine which artists are seen in museums. Powerful dealers are influential with museum directors. It is vital for artists and the art world that dealers exist. I believe that it is in the best interest of the artists, over the length of a career, to be represented by dealers.

My education in contemporary art had come primarily from dealers in prominent galleries. They were often more knowledgeable—and more willing to share their knowledge—than museum curators. They helped me train my eye to detect the best work being done in America. There were times when I was a gallery's best customer and its most ardent student.

About 95 percent of my collection was bought through dealers. As an avid collector, I have dealt with scores of dealers.

As I mentioned, when I did my major buying, the gallery got one-third of the purchase price the artist got two-thirds. Today it is often 60 percent to the gallery and 40 percent to the artist.

It is much more expensive to mount a show today than it was in the mid-1900s. Advertising costs have soared. Rents are high, even though artists and galleries are constantly searching for low-rent neighborhoods. Often artists find new places and the galleries follow. In recent years, we have seen the art scene move from SoHo, once a low-rent district, to Chelsea in Manhattan and Williamsburg in Brooklyn.

But the role of the dealer continues to be important. People love going to galleries, and enjoy the art they buy from knowledgeable, sensitive dealers.

Gallery owners are extremely important to the careers of the artists they represent. We might have known nothing about some of the greatest artists of our time had they not had dealers who believed in them and worked tirelessly to see that they reached the audience they deserved.

Dealers are equally important to collectors. Some gallery owners were my teachers, some were also my friends, many were characters who added spice to my life. Because I was collecting works by living artists, not old masters or even Impressionists, the galleries I visited were run generally by avant garde dealers, more creative and adventurous than owners of the more traditional, conservative galleries.

EDITH HALPERT AND THE DOWNTOWN GALLERY

Bright, charming, and attractive, Edith Halpert was one of the earliest advocates of twentieth-century American artists. She opened the Downtown Gallery on West Thirteenth Street in Greenwich Village in 1926, showing contemporary art five years before the Whitney opened on West Eighth Street.

Edith was born in Odessa, Ukraine, in 1900. She came to America at the age of six. When she was eighteen, she married Sam Halpert, an American artist, shown at the Metropolitan, who died quite young. When I met Edith, she was a youthful widow already well established as a dealer.

By the 1940s, the Downtown Gallery was equal in quality to far more famous American galleries. Edith was a superb saleswoman, passionately supportive of her artists.

For more than two decades, I bought an enormous amount from Edith, works of twenty different artists, including Jack Levine in 1943 and George L. K. Morris in 1944.

In 1944, I also went to Edith's Downtown Gallery for Horace Pippin's only New York show. Pippin was a great African-American, self-taught primitive painter, the most natural of the American primitives, a sharp contrast to Grandma Moses, whom I consider an excellent maker of color reproductions, but not an artist. I had no problem choosing Pippin's *Cabin in the Cotton*. I don't know how many people bought at his show but I'm glad that I did. Pippin died within two years.

I consider Pippin to be the closest American artist to Rousseau. He suffered from a permanent shoulder injury, inflicted in World War I, so he could use only one arm. Fortunately, I loaned *Cabin in the Cotton* to the 1944 exhibit *Painting in the United States* at the Carnegie Institute in Pittsburgh, where it earned Pippin his only prize.

When I bought Arthur Dove's *Holbrook's Bridge to the Northwest* from Edith Halpert in 1950, I knew that it was a really fabulous painting. It is hanging right now in my living room. Unlike most of my purchases in those years, this one does not show me as a collector of promising artists. He was already a sure thing.

I waited a long time for a really great Dove, and when I saw *Holbrook's Bridge*, I felt, as I still feel today, that it is an impeccable picture, close to being absolutely perfect. The simple composition, the blending of colors is equal to anything I have ever seen.

The painting is reproduced in Frederick S. Wight's *Arthur G. Dove* (University of California Press, Berkeley and Los Angeles, 1958, illustrated p. 72). Wight said of it: "It is rich, solemn, and steeped in the connotations which the word or symbol 'bridge' holds for painters, a passage from here to somewhere else, from now to the future."

But I really don't need confirmation from others on this one. My admiration for it has never wavered. I have loaned it many times— MoMA borrowed it for at least one exhibition—but it has usually been in my sight and always in my consciousness.

The following year, I bought works by Hans Hofmann and Joseph Stella at the Downtown Gallery. I also bought from Edith two watercolors by John Marin, who was still alive, both scenes of Maine: *In Maine* in 1948 and *Sea and Rocks, Mt. Desert, Maine* in 1950. In 1964 I acquired from Edith Max Weber's *La Parisienne*, painted in Paris in 1907.

I saw Edith often. Her high spirits and enthusiasm for art and artists made her good company.

The Downtown Gallery moved in and out of several locations, going further uptown each time. The last move was to East Fifty-first Street, far from downtown. But, by that time, the Downtown Gallery was well-known and Edith kept the name.

I gave Edith some advice on her last move. An opportunity arose for her to buy the building that housed her gallery on East Fifty-first Street. Edith was unsure what to do. She was a successful art dealer, not a real estate professional. I strongly urged her to buy the building, and she did. It became extremely valuable. Today, it is part of the Helmsley Hotel.

It was my good fortune to acquire from Edith the two Ben Shahn paintings, first *India*, and later *The Blind Accordion Player*, which was shown in a major Ben Shahn exhibition at the Jewish Museum in 1998. A story often told is that this painting was inspired by the celebrated photograph of a heartbroken accordionist playing during the departure of President Roosevelt's funeral cortege from Warm Springs, Georgia. But I saw qualities in the painting that transcended the particular moment of national grief. It carried Shahn far beyond anything that even the most powerful poster-maker could produce.

During the 1998 Shahn exhibition, a *New York Times* critic wrote that it was time for a reassessment of Shahn. He said Shahn was tied to his era's social and political events, more a leftist propagandist than a significant painter. At least, that was my interpretation of a somewhat mean-spirited article.

The great European palaces are filled with politically inspired art. Look at Versailles. No art could be more political than the paintings in the interrogation room of the Doge's Palace in Venice, where the interrogators are deified.

The *Times* review also put me in mind of a conversation with my old Paris friend, Meyer Schapiro, a giant among academics in the art world whose knowledge of Romanesque art was first rate, but who also knew a great deal about modern art.

I once asked Meyer, "How do you rate Ben Shahn versus Milton Avery?"

He said, "With great ease. Shahn is much better than Avery." The present world would argue with this. Today, Avery has a higher artistic reputation than Shahn. It is apparent in the marketplace, where an Avery now commands a much higher price than a Ben Shahn.

Nonetheless, I think Shahn's name will survive as the nearest thing to Daumier, an artist as a social commentator, although I would classify Daumier as a better painter.

Edith also represented Wood Gaylor, who had exhibited in the historic 1913 Armory Show. In 1930, before I began serious collecting, Edith gave Gaylor his first one-man exhibit. I didn't see this show. It wasn't until 1963, when the Munson-Williams-Proctor Institute in Utica, New York, mounted a reconstruction of the Armory Show, that I first encountered Gaylor's paintings. Long after the Downtown Gallery closed, I bought at the Zabriskie Gallery two charming Gaylors, each depicting an actual event in Greenwich Village, one a cocktail party, the other a birthday celebration. Edith Halpert knew the importance of Gaylor more than three decades before I did. She was ahead of most people most of the time.

ALFRED STIEGLITZ AT 291 FIFTH AVENUE

During the 1930s, when I was a young man doing more learning than buying, I went to An American Place at 291 Fifth Avenue, one of the best known galleries in the country, owned by the photographers Alfred Stieglitz and Edward Steichen.

Stieglitz operated brilliantly in a number of directions. He represented leading foreign artists as well as Americans. He was a painter and an extraordinary photographer.

When I went to his gallery, Stieglitz looked me over and virtually threw me out. He assumed that this skinny kid would never buy a picture. I was young and didn't look as if I had either the taste or the money.

I never went back. He gave me the feeling that I could never buy anything from him, and I never did.

After Stieglitz died in 1946, the artists he represented moved en masse to Edith Halpert. She inherited nearly the entire Stieglitz group. Since they were now represented by Edith at the Downtown Gallery, and not by Stieglitz, I was able to buy John Marin, Arthur Dove, and Max Weber.

Stieglitz was married to an extraordinary woman, Georgia O'Keeffe. I bought O'Keeffe's *Lake George by Early Moonrise* not from Stieglitz nor from Edith Halpert, who represented O'Keeffe later, but from Albert Duveen, a nephew of the great Lord Duveen.

Although it was a good decision to buy the O'Keeffe, it was an odd purchase for me. I don't know how Duveen acquired the painting. The original owner was O'Keeffe's physician, who had an estate on Lake George in upstate New York. The picture is highly romantic, full of subtle colors creating a dreamy atmosphere. O'Keeffe is not noted for romanticism, so it is an unusual Georgia O'Keeffe, which is one of the things that appealed to me about it. It was done early in her life, when she lived in New York.

The painting never became as famous as it would have been had I bought it from Edith Halpert or Stieglitz. Both dealers knew how to bring attention to a great work of art. Albert Duveen just happened to have bought this particular painting. He wasn't noted as being particularly interested in Georgia O'Keeffe.

My own opinion is that Georgia O'Keeffe was an extraordinary artist, but she is not as good as her reputation, which was in part the result of her connection with Alfred Stieglitz and the fact that she moved to New Mexico and painted well into her old age. She was a survivor.

She painted the Lake George picture just before Stieglitz took a number of nude photographs of her that were exhibited at the Metropolitan Museum. Very beautiful pictures. Very beautiful woman at that time, in fact at all times. In old age, she was still beautiful.

Stieglitz was a first-rate photographer, but not known much for his paintings. As a great dealer, he brought over outstanding artists from Europe. There is no question about his genius, although it is hard for me to say too much that is nice about someone who kicked me out of his gallery.

PEGGY GUGGENHEIM

Many people, including the energetic art dealer Sidney Janis, took credit for discovering Jackson Pollock. That is understandable because Pollock was around New York "undiscovered" for years, working on the WPA artists project, studying with Thomas Hart Benton, painting in Greenwich Village.

It was actually Peggy Guggenheim who believed that Pollock was a great painter. She displayed his paintings long before anyone else gave him recognition. Her gallery represented him and featured him in several shows. It was at Peggy Guggenheim's gallery that I first became familiar with Pollock's work.

Pollock was rumored to be badly in need of money. As a result, he made a rather strange deal with Peggy Guggenheim: She gave him a monthly sum—$250 or $300—and in exchange she owned all his paintings, except for one each year. He was so destitute that he made this deal. I thought it was a rather poor bargain.

At the outbreak of World War II, Peggy was living in Europe. She became a supporter of the Emergency Rescue Committee, headed by Varian Fry, a brave and imaginative young man who helped many intellectuals, musicians, and artists escape from Nazi-occupied France, including Marc Chagall, Jean Arp, Jacques Lipschitz, and Wassily Kandinsky. Working with Fry, Peggy paid passage to America for the family of Andre Breton and for the leading surrealist painter Max Ernst.

Peggy left Europe one step ahead of the Nazis. She lived in New York during the war, and befriended many American artists. Max Ernst became her husband for a short and turbulent time. Peggy opened a gallery on Fifty-seventh Street called Art of This Century. I went there, but not often enough. I didn't buy anything from her. No question that I should have paid much more attention to her than I did.

Over the years, Peggy Guggenheim's artistic judgment has been borne out. Her reputation has grown as an important person in twentieth-century art, especially in helping artists. She was quite sincere in her devotion to artists.

At the time, however, I didn't think of her as a serious art dealer. Stories of her outlandish sexual escapades drowned out any objective appreciation of her. Many people, and I'm afraid I was one, greatly underrated her. I thought she was wacky.

Peggy was usually described as a flamboyant woman, not beautiful but flamboyant. The wealthy and uninhibited life she lived is more often thought of in connection with Venice rather than New York. I visited her in Venice after the war. She had become a sad and bizarre case.

Although Peggy was a wealthy woman who devoted her life to art, she was often so frugal as to be stingy. Stories abounded of bad food at her parties, her bickering with brilliant but needy artists about a few dollars on the purchase price of a painting, and other miserly behavior by this extremely rich lady.

Despite these personal shortcomings, she really was one of the most important and sophisticated art dealers of her time. Many of us didn't give her enough credit.

BETTY PARSONS

When Peggy Guggenheim returned to Europe after the war, she closed her gallery, Art of This Century. She had a lot of trouble finding another gallery for Jackson Pollock because of his reputation as a heavy drinker. Betty Parsons was finally persuaded to represent him.

Betty was an artist herself, briefly married to an artist, and among the best of the early dealers. She and Edith Halpert presided over galleries showing the work of living American artists much earlier than most dealers. Betty's artists were devoted to her.

Because I liked Betty and respected her judgment, I went to the November 1949 opening of the Jackson Pollock show at her gallery. The previous summer, *Life* magazine had run an article about Pollock that asked, "Is he the greatest living painter in the United States?" The article evoked considerable interest and debate, which was reflected in the huge turnout. I liked what I saw that evening, and told Betty that I did.

A few days later, she called me. I remember the words: "Roy, you know that painting you liked in the Jackson Pollock show? Would you entertain buying it? He needs money desperately."

"Yes," I said and I sent off the check in advance of getting the painting so Pollock would have the money right away.

The painting I bought, now in the Neuberger Museum of Art, is *Number 8, 1949*, a fine example of Pollock's groundbreaking poured paintings. Measuring almost 6 feet by 3 feet, covered with green, red, yellow, and aluminum-colored paint interspersed with large black lines, the picture radiates great strength and energy. It has been exhibited extensively in shows throughout the country. To my mind, it is one of Pollock's best works.

Although I was told at the time that my check enabled Pollock to heat his house in Springs, near East Hampton, Long Island, it has since been reported that he was not quite so desperate for money, and that he only presented himself as impoverished. He was spending a lot of money on renovating his house. One way or another, I helped make his home a little more comfortable, and I am glad about that.

Having seen Pollock's early work at Peggy Guggenheim's and later in other galleries and museums, I felt I knew his art completely. By the time I bought *Number 8* from Betty Parsons, I was quite familiar with his art and comfortable with my purchase. I first met Jackson Pollock at the 1949 show, and later ran into him from time to time at the Cedar Tavern, a café on University Place in Greenwich Village, near New York University, that was popular with artists. I never got to know him the way I did Ben Shahn, Milton Avery, or the sculptor David Smith, also a big drinker who died early.

Pollock died at forty-four in 1956 in a terrible accident when he was driving drunk. A woman in the car with him also died. I am not a fan of the automobile, and these senseless deaths of young geniuses just add to that feeling.

Shortly after the Pollock tragedy, I acquired *Burning Candles*, a collage by Pollock's wife Lee Krasner, but the purchase had nothing to do with the death of her husband. I was impressed by her use of a medium that I had always viewed with suspicion. Lee Krasner's first one-artist exhibition had been at the Betty Parsons Gallery in 1950, the year after her husband's show.

Although I did not buy *Burning Candles* from Betty, I did acquire paintings from her by a number of different artists, including two by Hedda Sterne.

Betty Parsons and I were once asked by my friend Charlie Cunningham, director of the distinguished Wadsworth Atheneum in Hartford, Connecticut, to appear together on a television program about contemporary art. Hartford is a medium-sized city dominated by insurance companies. It might not appear to be the ideal site for a museum that is almost as encyclopedic as the Met and as devoted to contemporary art as the Museum of Modern Art. But there is the Wadsworth, in the shadow of the state capitol at Hartford.

It was typical of Charlie Cunningham that he would encourage people in Connecticut to be involved in the world of living American artists by putting an ardent collector like me and a superb professional like Betty on television.

On the train to Connecticut, I saw that Betty was very nervous. "What are you nervous about?" I asked her. "You know your subject better than any of the viewers."

I might have added that if anyone should be nervous, it was me. But my passion for art is so great that I love sharing it. For me, speaking about art has always been a pleasure.

The show went well, and we both felt good about it. Betty was very shy about herself, but comfortable talking about her artists, which she did with skill and enthusiasm.

In 1977, I saw Betty at a MoMA party where Alfred Barr was given an award. She was well into her seventies and she looked very youthful and absolutely stunning. I complimented her on how beautiful she looked and, more generally, on her creativity in life.

Betty was always a creative, adventuresome person. She was not the greatest dealer from a business standpoint, but she was a tremendous influence from an aesthetic and a human point of view.

OTHER POLLOCK CHAMPIONS:
SIDNEY JANIS AND EUGENE THAW

Sidney Janis, an important Pollock aficionado, began his career not as an art dealer but as a collector who made money in the shirt business. He was still a good tennis player in his seventies and an ardent dancer who went three evenings a week to the Roseland dance hall. He was a sharp businessman with strong opinions.

Sidney was correct in a great many of his judgments. In 1933, he bought several Paul Klees and a large primitive painting, *The Dream*, by Henri Rousseau. It is a masterpiece. A Rousseau painting is rare and very valuable. Ultimately, Nelson Rockefeller bought the painting from Janis for the Museum of Modern Art, where it has been prominently displayed and much admired. By 1935, Janis had a collection large and important enough to be shown at the MoMA.

Janis was one of several well-known collectors who ultimately became dealers. He opened his gallery in 1948, fairly late in the history of American contemporary art. Edith Halpert, Betty Parsons, Valentine Dudensing, Curt Valentin, J. B. Neumann—all excellent people whom I dealt with—had been in business for quite a while when Sidney started out.

Sidney created a stir with his choice of a location for his new gallery—in the same building, on the same floor, as Betty Parsons, much to her unhappiness. They were not friendly. He was much more promotion-minded than Betty or any of the other early dealers. Often artists leave their dealers in favor of someone they believe can do more for their careers. This happened in several cases with artists coming to Janis.

Janis was successful in attracting both American and European major artists. His gallery opened with an exhibition of Fernand Leger, and soon acquired many works by Piet Mondrian.

Jackson Pollock joined Janis. So did Arp, de Kooning, and Motherwell. Mark Rothko, whom I originally met at Milton Avery's home, was one of the artists who went from Peggy Guggenheim to Betty Parsons and then to Sidney Janis. In 1957, I bought Rothko's warm and mysterious painting, *Old Gold Over White*, from Janis.

Sidney's gallery was very simple and quite small. But the catalogues he produced were spectacular and influential. He used expensive paper and often reproduced the art in colors as close to the originals as possible. He also included photos of previous exhibitions. Sidney was extremely clever in his use of visual material. The Sidney Janis Gallery still exists, run by one of his sons. It is still a fine gallery.

Jackson Pollock had another fan among dealers, a man who was more scholar than promoter: the remarkable Eugene Thaw, whom I rank high in any evaluation of dealers. I learned a great deal from him.

I enjoyed hearing Thaw lecture to small audiences at the Morgan Library. Once he spoke about Pollock's drawings. He showed a screen with a Pollock on one side and an old master—I think it was Rembrandt—on the other side. Thaw demonstrated visually in detail how good an artist Pollock was. Only a few years earlier, people were laughing at Jackson Pollock. Thaw took him very seriously.

Thaw did not represent artists in the usual way. He bought their paintings. Sometimes he sold them, sometimes he kept them for himself. I bought half a dozen excellent works from him, all small, all of high quality.

Eugene Thaw and Clare, his wife, gave a substantial collection, mostly drawings, to the Morgan Library. Among them is a pen-and-ink drawing dashed off by Rembrandt. In June 1999, the Thaws made a farsighted gift of $10 million for the conservation and preservation of works on paper.

This kind of gift was characteristic of Thaw. It is being used to preserve the Library's holdings of important works on paper (musical manuscripts, books, and drawings such as Paul Cezanne's *Bathers*) and to train a new generation of conservators for the Morgan and other institutions.

Eugene Thaw, as dealer, scholar, and innovative philanthropist, is a leader in the art world for whom I have enormous respect.

TWO LEGENDS: PAUL ROSENBERG AND VALENTINE DUDENSING

Paul Rosenberg was a member of a huge, wealthy, well-respected Parisian family of dealers in antiques, silver, and art. The first Rosenberg gallery opened in Paris in 1878.

Paul was not a handsome man, but he was bright and rich both in money and in Degas and Picasso canvasses. When he came to America shortly before World War II, he opened a gorgeous gallery on Fifty-seventh Street. During the 1940s, he ran one of the three especially distinguished galleries in New York. The others were the Wildenstein and the old Knoedler.

In France, Paul specialized in well-known European painters. In America, he decided to include only a few American artists. Among those he chose were Milton Avery, Marsden Hartley, Max Weber, and Abraham Rattner.

I became friendly with Paul and interested in his artists. In 1943, he showed me the work of Marsden Hartley and I purchased what may be the best-known painting in my collection, Hartley's *Fishermen's Last Supper*. When I brought it home, I felt that I now had an American masterpiece.

Also in 1943, I bought Abraham Rattner's romantic *April Showers* from Paul Rosenberg, a painting I like so much it still hangs prominently in my apartment. It was reproduced in *Town and Country* magazine the year after I acquired it but Rattner's colors are so wonderful that the original is a different experience. The multiple renderings of the woman and her umbrella create a gentle, wistful mood. The abstract quality of the painting, which helps create that mood, is a reflection of the time. Rattner became more of an abstract expressionist in his later works.

In 1945, I bought Max Weber's *String Music* from Paul Rosenberg, a stirring painting of three musicians that reflects Weber at his best.

When Paul was about to retire, I bought a great number of Milton Avery paintings from him. On a single day I purchased over fifty Averys.

Rosenberg was the second dealer to represent Avery. He bought a whole block of Milton's work for very little money. Within a month after I bought *Gaspé Landscape* from Milton at his studio, I paid Paul Rosenberg only $350 for a framed Avery, *Girl in a Wicker Chair, 1944,* a painting of Milton's daughter, March Avery. Both paintings are still home with me.

Milton Avery's earliest dealer, Valentine Dudensing, was a handsome man with a great eye for art, one of the wisest dealers of the twentieth century. He taught me to turn paintings upside down when judging them. If they were good upside down, it was a verification of their composition. For some reason, it worked.

Dudensing had an enormous impact in developing American interest in contemporary art. He had great artistic judgment and foresight. In 1933, when they were not fully recognized as artists, he championed works by Derain, Matisse, Picasso, Modigliani, Braque, Mondrian, Kandinsky, and Miro. Val began representing Avery when hardly anyone had heard of him. He recognized the French influence in Avery's work.

Although Val exhibited many more Europeans than Americans, I bought a lot from the Valentine Gallery and had tremendous respect for him. Among the Americans the gallery represented, in addition to Milton Avery, were Louis Eilshemius, Joseph Stella, and Raphael Soyer.

Val's father was a New York art dealer who ran a rather traditional gallery. While in Europe to study art, the young Dudensing met Pierre Matisse, the son of my favorite European artist. They arranged for Dudensing to open a New York gallery that would be stocked with modern art from France supplied by Pierre Matisse. This arrangement lasted a few years. When I met Dudensing in the 1930s his gallery (founded in 1926) was well-established and he had his own relationships with artists, particularly with Picasso.

Dudensing had great influence on Alfred Barr, the first director of the Museum of Modern Art, and on the artistic direction of MoMA. Most of Dudensing's artists are represented in the MoMA collection. Barr's judgment was that Dudensing might well be the greatest dealer.

Max Weber, *la Parisienne,* 1907, oil on canvas. (Photo by Jim Frank.)

Lyonel Feininger, *High Houses II,* 1913, oil on canvas. (© 2002 Artists Rights Society [ARS], New York/VG Bild-Kunst, Bonn. Photo by Jim Frank.)

Stuart Davis, *Barber Shop,* 1930, oil on canvas. (© Estate of Stuart Davis/Licensed by VAGA, New York. Photo by Jim Frank.)

Georgia O'Keeffe, *Lake George by Early Moonrise,* 1930, oil and gouache on canvas. (© 2002 The Georgia O'Keeffe Foundation/Artists Rights Society [ARS], New York. Photo by Jim Frank.)

Edward Hopper, *Barber Shop,* 1931, oil on canvas. (Courtesy Neuberger Museum of Art. Photo by Jim Frank.)

Arthur Dove, *Holbrook's Bridge to the Northwest,* 1938, oil on canvas. (Photo by Jim Frank.)

Marsden Hartley, *Fishermen's Last Supper,* 1940–41, oil on canvas. (Photo by Jim Frank.)

Milton Avery, *Self-Portrait,* 1941, oil on canvas. (© 2002 Milton Avery Trust/Artists Rights Society [ARS], New York. Photo by Jim Frank.)

Jack Levine, *The Banquet,* 1941, oil on canvas. (© Jack Levine/Licensed by VAGA, New York. Photo by Jim Frank.)

Milton Avery, *Gaspé Landscape,* 1942–43, oil on canvas. (© 2002 Milton Avery Trust/Artists Rights Society [ARS], New York. Photo by Jim Frank.)

Alexander Calder, Untitled (Male and Female), 1944, gouache on paper.
(© 2002 Estate of Alexander Calder/Artists Rights Society [ARS], New York.
Photo by Jim Frank.)

Horace Pippin, *Cabin in the Cotton III*, 1944, oil on canvas. (Courtesy Neuberger Museum
of Art. Photo by Jim Frank.)

David Smith, *The Billiard Player,* 1945, steel. (© Estate of David Smith/Licensed by VAGA, New York. Photo by Jim Frank.)

Ben Shahn, *The Blind Accordion Player,* 1945, tempera on board. (© Ben Shahn / Licensed by VAGA, New York. Photo by Jim Frank.)

John Marin, *Sea and Rocks, Mt. Desert, Maine,* 1948, watercolor on canvas. (© 2002 Estate of John Marin/Artists Rights Society [ARS], New York. Photo by Jim Frank.)

Jackson Pollock, *Number 8, 1949,* 1949, oil, enamel and aluminum paint on canvas. (© 2002 Pollock-Krasner Foundation/Artists Rights Society [ARS], New York. Photo by Jim Frank.)

Hans Hofmann, *Fruit Bowl, Version 6*, 1950, oil on canvas. (© 2002 Estate of Hans Hofmann/Artists Rights Society [ARS], New York. Photo by Jim Frank.)

Willem de Kooning, *Marilyn Monroe,* 1954, oil on canvas. (© 2002 The Willem
de Kooning Foundation/Artists Rights Society [ARS], New York. Photo by Jim Frank.)

Richard Diebenkorn, *Girl on Terrace*, 1956, oil on canvas. (© The Estate of Richard Diebenkorn. Photo by Jim Frank.)

Mark Rothko, *Old Gold Over White,* 1956, oil on canvas. (© 1998 Kate Rothko Prizel & Christopher Rothko/Artists Rights Society [ARS], New York. Photo by Jim Frank.)

Romare Bearden, *Melon Season*, 1967, paper collage on canvas. (© Romare Bearden Foundation/Licensed by VAGA, New York. Photo by Jim Frank.)

Henry Moore, *Large Two Forms,* 1966–69, bronze. (Photo by Jim Frank. With the permission of the Henry Moore Foundation.)

Abraham Rattner, *April Showers,* 1939, oil on canvas. (Photo by Jim Frank.)

Picasso's masterpiece *Guernica*, his monumental rendering of the horrors of the Spanish Civil War, was first shown at the Valentine Gallery. Through Dudensing's relationships with both Picasso and Barr, it was arranged that *Guernica* be displayed at the Modern Museum until the death of the Spanish dictator Francisco Franco. The powerful antiwar mural hung at MoMA for fifty years. Now that Franco is dead and Spain is again a free country, *Guernica* hangs in the Princess Sophia Museum in Madrid.

In 1947, when he was only fifty-five, Val Dudensing decided to close his gallery and move to France. Two years later he came back to empty his warehouse, and again I bought an entire inventory of Milton Avery paintings. It was one of the best things I ever did. I acquired forty-six Averys in one day.

Before buying the Averys in large quantity, I checked with Sally Avery, who advised Milton on practical matters. I asked her how they would feel about a big purchase. They were delighted.

I checked because if you own a large number of an artist's works, you influence his career. I know cases where such ownership was detrimental to the artist, where someone could compete in the market with the artist's attempt to sell later works.

At the same time as the Avery purchases, I foolishly spurned Val's offer of a Picasso Harlequin sculpture that I was crazy about and that he offered to me for $1,500. At the time, I thought of myself as a collector of American art, which I now realize was a too-rigid classification. I was actually interested in the work of living artists no matter where they were born. A lot of European artists were living in America. I didn't pay any attention to citizenship. In 1944, I bought *Woman Spinning*, a painting by the Mexican artist Rufino Tamayo who was living in New York City and teaching at the Dalton School. He was not an American citizen.

I was among the last to bid the Dudensings farewell when Val and his wife moved permanently to the French countryside, where he lived for the last twenty years of his life.

SAMUEL KOOTZ AND LEO CASTELLI

Samuel Kootz opened his gallery on Madison Avenue immediately after World War II. In a sense, I was his earliest backer. Shortly after the gallery opened, he said, "Roy, I do not have a big mailing list. May I have an exhibition of works from your collection?" I said yes. It was understood that although the paintings would be exhibited, they were not for sale. The show was well-publicized. One magazine devoted a half-dozen pages to it. People who attended signed in, so it did increase Sam's mailing list. His gallery became quite successful.

Sam wrote a brilliant book on art, which I read very carefully. He knew a great deal about the subject. I made several purchases from him. The first was Stuart Davis' great painting, *Barber Shop*, in 1942. I paid $250 for that terrific Stuart Davis. In 1942, $250 was a lot of money. Two years later, I bought from Sam the Calder gouache untitled by the artist but known as *Male and Female*. Over the years, I also bought Hans Hofmann's *Fruit Bowl*, Carl Holty's *Carousel*, and Byron Browne's *Trombone Solo* from the Kootz Gallery.

Many previously unknown artists were brought to public attention by Sam. I had great confidence in his taste, though he turned down Jackson Pollock and David Smith because of their drinking.

In 1949, Sam became a dealer for Picasso. He obtained nine large Picasso canvases that he showed in Dallas at the Nieman Marcus department store. That was the beginning of art awareness in Texas.

The Samuel M. Kootz Gallery made Madison Avenue the uptown place to be. It was soon joined by Hirschl & Adler, Perls, David Findlay, Leo Castelli, and many other galleries.

Castelli, a dapper, elegant man, was born in Italy and lived for some years in France before settling in New York. In 1957, he opened a Madison Avenue gallery with a show of leading European and American painters. Although he later moved the bulk of his business downtown to SoHo, Castelli maintained a presence on Madison Avenue.

During his first year of operation, I bought six works from Castelli, including Marisol's *Queen,* a charming bust that revealed a genuinely individual talent. I like it better than some of her later work, which, to my eye, became too cute. I also bought from Castelli an early abstract painting by Morris Louis, one of three paintings that fortunately had survived Louis' deliberate destruction of much of his own work.

The painting shows Louis' restless energy. Its color and its adventurous feeling still captivate me. I was on the verge of buying another one and didn't do it. That was a mistake. But you can't buy everything.

THE ART WORLD CHANGES

A year later, I went back to Castelli and everything had changed. The art world had changed. I didn't recognize a single artist in his gallery.

Leo Castelli became a leading figure in the Post-Abstract Expressionist avant garde. Among the talented people he represented were Frank Stella, Robert Rauschenberg, Roy Lichtenstein, Jasper Johns, and Andrew Warhol, some of whom arouse my skepticism. Warhol, for instance, was an extremely interesting man, but I question if he is an enduring artist. I wonder how people will rate him 100 years from now.

The same month I returned to Leo Castelli's gallery, I received a phone call from Victor Ganz, one of the largest collectors of Picasso. The price for Picasso had gone too high even for him. He had moved to American art and tried to convince me to buy a Jasper Johns for $200 or $300. I didn't do it. Forty years later, Si Newhouse, the publisher, paid $17 million for a Jasper Johns.

My return visit to Leo Castelli's confirmed my thinking that the art world had been transformed. Promotion-minded gallery owners were bringing public attention to living artists—those who were really good and deserved the attention, and also some of the Pop and Minimal artists I deemed of questionable value, selling at what seemed to me highly inflated prices. I felt that contemporary American art had become subject to excessive speculation and market manipulation.

For two decades, I had been collecting works by living artists, mostly living American artists. My collection of paintings and sculptures gave me great pleasure, as did my involvement with museums and with the American Federation of Arts. I am proud of the number of important careers that were advanced not only through my own acquisitions but also through the museums I was able to persuade to buy and exhibit works of living artists, and through the traveling art shows of the AFA.

With Castelli, Janis, and a new breed of promoters at work, I learned that many artists were doing so well they didn't need me. After twenty years, I decided to free myself from the limitation of time and place constraints. Though I remained interested in the work of living artists, I began collecting whatever appealed to me, regardless of when it was created. I began buying some ancient art, which I love, and roaming a bit more freely.

TODAY'S GALLERIES

When I began collecting, New York City galleries were in Greenwich Village or on Fifty-seventh Street. This was a time when artists and galleries were located all over the Village, before high-rise apartment buildings and high-rent commercial ventures pushed artists to the East Village, then to SoHo, Tribeca, and Chelsea.

Today, there are hundreds of galleries all over the city. Sam Kootz opened Madison Avenue as the uptown place to be. We now have a thriving art scene in SoHo, Tribeca, Chelsea, out on the Hudson on the Chelsea Pier, Williamsburg in Brooklyn—just about everywhere. A few galleries still exist in the once avant garde East Village.

I still love going to galleries. Sometimes I find a new art show I can't resist. It's an incurable addiction. I am fond of the Maxwell Davidson Gallery, which exhibits the art to which I have devoted a lifetime—twentieth-century American masters, young artists of exceptional promise, and French Impressionists.

The Maxwell Davidson Gallery shows work by George Rickey and what might be called the Calder school of sculpture. In 1995, I bought a mahogany, steel, and bronze sculpture called *Flourishing Flywheel*, the work of a young artist, Pedro De Movellan. I went to see him again in 1999, and his work was still better. In the summer of 2000, I bought another of his sculptures as a ninetieth birthday present for Kitty Carlisle Hart. She is crazy about it.

I commend him to young people, the new collectors. I hope they will have great adventures getting to know the art being produced by their contemporaries in the twenty-first century.

Roy Neuberger and Kitty Carlisle Hart at a MoMA party. (Photo by Lynn Saville.)

CHAPTER FIVE

MOMA: MODERN ART COMES OF AGE

I was there, a young man of twenty-six, recently returned from living in Europe, when the Museum of Modern Art first opened its doors. It seemingly could not have happened at a worse time. Nine days earlier, on Black Tuesday, October 29, 1929, the stock market collapsed.

But even in the midst of financial bedlam, the new museum on the twelfth floor of the Heckscher Building on Fifth Avenue attracted more than 10,000 visitors a week, 47,000 during a four-week exhibit of four nineteenth-century giants—Paul Cezanne, Paul Gauguin, Georges Seurat, and Vincent van Gogh.

Here in America were the paintings I had fallen in love with in Paris. There was a sense of adventure at that opening, of being present at the birth of a dream. The exhibit heralded the direction that MoMA would take through the years: bringing the best of European art to American audiences.

Who would have dreamed, in those days of breadlines and foreclosures, how successful this venture would ultimately be, and how valuable the art shown by the Modern Museum would become. If anyone had told the art lovers and collectors at the Modern Museum in those early days that by the end of the century the paintings we liked would sell for many millions of dollars, he would have been dismissed as a nut.

The Modern Museum's second show, "Nineteen Living Americans," opened on December 13, 1929, and was more in the direction of my major interest, but the exhibit was something of a hodgepodge. It became more notable for the painters it left out than for the mixture of good and mediocre that was presented. There was nothing, for instance, by Charles Sheeler, Stuart Davis, or Arthur Dove, American painters whose works are in my collection and were also ultimately bought by the Modern Museum. America in 1929 was apparently not yet ready to deal with homegrown talent. The show was not greeted with enthusiasm.

In January 1930, the Museum of Modern Art again showed European artists and again attendance soared. In subsequent years, under the leadership of Dorothy Miller, the museum's curator of American art, MoMA put on significant shows of American artists. But its greatest successes, its blockbuster shows, focused heavily on importing the works of leading Europeans.

MoMA'S THREE DOTING MOTHERS AND A DISTANT FATHER

Abigail Aldrich Rockefeller, the wife of John D. Rockefeller Jr., one of America's richest men, was the mother hen of MoMA. Mrs. Rockefeller shared an enthusiasm for modern art with two friends, Lillie Bliss and Mary Sullivan. While some society ladies might meet for tea to plan a country club dance, these three conspired over tea in the top-floor art gallery in Abby Rockefeller's townhouse on West Fifty-fourth Street, discussing how to broaden the audience for the modern art they admired and collected.

John D. Rockefeller Jr. was a stern, deeply conservative, puritanical man who began to buy art only after he had been convinced by the great art dealer Joseph Duveen that it was morally acceptable and prudent to invest in beautiful objects, particularly when most of them would ultimately wind up in public institutions like the Metropolitan Museum. Rockefeller helped the Metropolitan build the magnificent Cloisters in upper Manhattan. He liked tapestries, porcelains, and rugs. He didn't care much for paintings, even superb old masters. Clearly, he was not a man to buy modern pictures by living artists.

When his wife Abigail began collecting modern art in the 1920s, John D. was much distressed. Not only did he dislike modern art, he was unhappy about his wife's devotion to it. He kept her on a tight art budget. Despite these constraints, Abby Rockefeller managed to put together a grand collection, most of which she eventually gave to MoMA.

By the spring of 1929, Abby Rockefeller and her two friends had resolved to establish a new museum. Lillie Bliss was one of the great early collectors who had been buying modern art since the 1913 Armory show. Her bequest, including nine Cezannes, would be the start of MoMA's permanent collection. Mary Sullivan was the art dealer from whom I bought Peter Hurd's *Boy from the Plains*, my first important acquisition.

MoMA'S FIRST PRESIDENT

It might have been judged unseemly in 1929 for three women to undertake such a venture as founding a new museum, so they invited

A. Conger Goodyear, a wealthy Buffalo collector, to join them and become president.

Goodyear had moved his business from Buffalo to New York City following a messy divorce and a minor art scandal. In Buffalo, as president of the Albright Art Gallery, he made an unauthorized purchase of an early Picasso painting, *La Toilette*. He bought it without consulting the Board of Trustees, who found it far too abstract. I saw it a few years later, exhibited at MoMA, on loan from the Albright. It is an extremely serene Picasso. But back in the 1920s, the trustees in Buffalo were so alarmed by this painting that they ousted Goodyear.

Conger Goodyear was delighted to become the first president of the new Museum of Modern Art. He held that post for a decade.

Yet, despite his deep involvement with MoMA, when it came time to decide the future of his own considerable collection, he astounded his colleagues in New York by announcing that all his art would go to Buffalo. By then, the Albright Gallery had expanded with a tremendous infusion of money and art from a group of supporters, notably my friend Shorty Knox, a very fine man. In 1962 it became the Albright-Knox Art Gallery.

The opening in Buffalo of a new wing to the art building and a new name was celebrated with a big dedication. It was my first visit to Buffalo—and to Niagara Falls, which I thought was big but not exciting. The gallery celebration was exciting because of the quality of the art. Albright-Knox had expanded into one of the finest collections of modern art anywhere.

I had a splendid time in Buffalo with Mr. Heinz (of the famous pickles) and with Alfred Barr, who told me that the Albright-Knox quality was better than MoMA, "But we are going to make it different," he said. And of course he did.

In 1964, after receiving the Goodyear collection, the Albright-Knox Art Gallery immediately auctioned it off.

ALFRED BARR: A BRILLIANT SCHOLAR FINDS HIS MISSION

Before MoMA could open its doors, the founders needed a director. For guidance they turned to Paul Sachs, who had left his father's investment firm, Goldman Sachs, to teach at Harvard. He gave the first course in America on museum management.

Sachs recommended a young protege, Alfred Barr, who had studied with him at Harvard and gone on to devise the first university course in modern art, which he taught at Wellesley College. This course ultimately become a model for an education program at MoMA.

In the summer of 1929, Abby Rockefeller interviewed Alfred Barr at her summer home in Seal Harbor, Maine. It was the beginning of an important professional relationship and deep personal friendship that lasted until her death in 1948.

Appointing the twenty-seven-year-old Barr as MoMA's first director was a brave and farsighted choice by the three women and their new president. Though academically proficient, Barr had no museum experience. But by the end of the summer in 1929, Barr was hard at work on the museum that would become the central passion of his life.

I got to know Alfred Barr when we were both young men setting out on new careers. He started at MoMA just a few months after I went to Wall Street. I began chatting with him during my visits to MoMA and we became friendly. Although I never served on the Board of MoMA—I was busy with Wall Street, my collection, the Whitney, the Met, and of course, the Neuberger Museum—I was always active in MoMA and contributed to expanding its collection. And I was happy to be a member of the International Council of the Museum.

Barr was serious, industrious, scholarly, and educated at Princeton and Harvard. You didn't have fun with him the way you did with Sandy Calder or with Barr's colleagues at MoMA, Jim Sweeney and Jim Soby. But his brilliance and sincerity were instantly apparent.

Barr transformed the definition of a museum by creating departments that had never been part of an art museum. He established exciting departments of architecture, prints, and a groundbreaking department of motion pictures. He was among the first to view cinema as an art form, and to devote museum space and intelligent comment and evaluation to it. His decision to include a library within the museum was of tremendous importance in developing educational programs.

He originated what became a great photography department and brought in as director Beaumont Newhall, another Paul Sachs' alumnus. Newhall was succeeded by Edward Steichen.

Today, it is commonplace to have such a department. I originally thought that photography was more a commercial thing and not a great art form. Perhaps I was wrong. Photography as an art form is widely accepted today.

Barr's inclusion of architecture, photography, motion pictures, and prints brought new perspectives to the role of a museum.

Alfred was a sophisticated writer and speaker who also was able to put together a superb staff. I think MoMA became preeminent because it had excellent scholars. Outstanding intellectuals came to MoMA from the Fogg Museum at Harvard, the Institute of Fine Arts in Chicago, and other prominent museums. Many of the people on the staff of MoMA, Barr appointees like James Soby and Dorothy Miller, didn't think of themselves as scholars, but they were.

Even in American art, MoMA in its own way did a better job than the Whitney, primarily because of Dorothy Miller's first-class shows of American art, starting in 1941 and into the 1950s.

Barr was more interested in European art than in what was happening in America. His focus on Picasso, Matisse, Braque, Miro, and other Europeans was reflected in the direction the museum took. It was Barr who first introduced American audiences to the work of Picasso and Matisse.

Alfred wrote wonderful biographies of both artists. He also wrote a short volume published by MoMA that has sold millions of copies—*What Is Modern Painting?*

He had a splendid teammate: his wife Margaret ("Marga" or "Daisy") Scolari-Fitzmaurice, half-Italian, half-Irish, fluent in many languages and herself an excellent art scholar. Marga was studying art history at New York University at the time of MoMA's opening exhibit, where she met Barr. They married the following year and immediately set off on the first of many summers in Europe that proved to be terrifically important to the museum. The Barrs met with leading artists and museum people, and unearthed, identified, and acquired some of the major paintings of the twentieth century. Marga worked as hard as Alfred on these trips, although MoMA did not even pay her expenses.

In the mid-1950s, I gave Alfred Barr some money to buy contemporary American art. I had no influence in how the museum spent this money, but of course I was curious. Alfred told me that MoMA bought half a dozen paintings, including a Lee Gatch, with the funds I gave them. I enthusiastically agreed with this choice. I like Gatch so much that I own three of his paintings. I am especially fond of *The Greenhouse*, an abstract painting I acquired in 1950, the year it was created. Some critics consider it one of the most important paintings of the 1950s.

Barr also told me that some of the money was used to obtain a Hedda Sterne abstract painting. Unfamiliar with her work, I went to the Betty Parsons Gallery for a look, I liked what I saw, and I bought an abstraction by Sterne—my most adventurous acquisition of that time—for my own collection.

In this purchase, I was strongly influenced by Alfred Barr. Usually, I made up my own mind about what to buy, based on judgments honed in viewing art, reading, talking to dealers, museum people, other collectors, and the artists themselves. It is especially interesting to hear what artists have to say about one another.

I also kept an eye on my mentor Duncan Phillips. I didn't necessarily follow Duncan Phillips, but I learned about building a collection by watching him.

It is relatively easy to be a scholar of the past, like Barr's colleague at Princeton, Millard Meiss, who wrote brilliantly about the Florentine frescoes. It is much tougher to be a scholar of your own century and to make judgments about the work of your contemporaries. Later on, it becomes clearer which works are masterpieces.

No matter how much one learns about art of the past, it is risky and very speculative to make judgments about new artists. This has always been so, except perhaps for Italy in the Renaissance. The Medici may have known they had a sure thing when they bought Michelangelo.

From our vantage point now, early in the twenty-first century, it is more apparent how art of the twentieth century is valued and which artists produced work of lasting importance. Barr made this kind of judgment at the time, and he was almost always right.

Barr's influence made MoMA extremely important. Its own educational activities, carried out by a superb staff, often shattered tradition.

Even more important was the influence that radiated out from MoMA to museums throughout the country. During the turbulent mid-century years, especially in the 1940s and the 1950s, Barr became enormously powerful in the art world as an innovator, scholar, critic, teacher, and crusader for contemporary painting, sculpture, architecture, film, and photography.

He made the Museum of Modern Art the most important institution of its kind. His influence was reflected in every museum decision throughout the country. His greatest contribution, to my mind, was establishing a new model of a museum that has been followed all over the world.

In his beneficial influence, Alfred Barr ranks, in my judgment, as not only one of the most important Americans of the twentieth-century art world, but one of the most influential Americans in the twentieth century. This evaluation would not be unanimously endorsed. It was often said that Barr was a better scholar than administrator. He was indeed a great scholar of modern art.

Different things need to be done in the art world. Alfred was busy innovating, writing, lecturing, teaching, enhancing the museum's collection, and advising anyone lucky enough to receive the benefit of his knowledge and judgment.

THE EBULLIENT NELSON ROCKEFELLER

Although Abigail Rockefeller could not interest her husband in modern art, her children were a different matter. Under her guidance, her son Laurance became an art collector. So did David and Blanchette (wife of John D. III), who would both serve as presidents of MoMA.

It was Nelson, however, whose passionate and enthusiastic interest in art equaled his mother's and whose leadership at MoMA was unique.

Nelson was already an avid collector when he joined MoMA board in 1932 at the age of twenty-four. Seven years later, he succeeded Conger Goodyear as president.

Perhaps no other person in modern times with so many other things to do has made a greater contribution to the field of art than Nelson Rockefeller. His knowledge was great and his love of art even greater. He combined his mother's passion for modern art with a sense of realism about museum operation.

Nelson had broad interests. He collected modern painting and sculpture. He was fascinated by primitive art, and amassed a huge amount of it with the help of Rene d'Harnoncourt, who would succeed Barr as director of MoMA.

Rockefeller also was deeply involved in modern architecture. He was active in the choice of an architect when MoMA was planning its own building on West Fifty-third Street. He was disappointed that a cut-through north from Fifty-first Street, which would have had the new MoMA facing the end of Rockefeller Plaza, never materialized.

Later, when Rockefeller proposed to me that we establish a Neuberger Museum of Art at Purchase College, New York, it was clear from the outset that Philip Johnson, one of Nelson's favorite architects, would design the building.

It was through the Modern Museum that I first got to know Nelson Rockefeller. Shortly after he became president of MoMA, President Franklin D. Roosevelt asked him to put together an art show to send to South America as part of the Roosevelt-era Good Neighbor Policy. Nelson grew up knowing a lot about South America because the Rockefeller corporation, Standard Oil of New Jersey, had major interests in Venezuela and other Latin American countries. For the Good Neighbor art show, Nelson borrowed my Peter Hurd *Boy from the Plains*.

In developing his extensive collection of modern art, Nelson relied heavily on Alfred Barr and Dorothy Miller. Often on a Saturday afternoon, when I was visiting galleries, I would encounter this trio, sometimes on the trail of a painting that also interested me. Although I bought a lot of art, Rockefeller's buying tremendously outstripped mine. He put together an enormous collection.

Other collectors, especially members of MoMA Board of Trustees, also relied on Barr's advice. Sometimes they used him to help mold their buying in the way that earlier collectors relied on Lord Duveen. Olga Guggenheim (an aunt of Peggy Guggenheim who was wealthier than Peggy) sought Barr's guidance on spending really large sums, particularly on Picassos.

Nelson Rockefeller sometimes bought the works of artists included in MoMA's new talent exhibitions of American art and in larger exhibitions curated by Dorothy Miller.

While he was governor, Rockefeller gave much of his art to New York State. It is displayed in government buildings in Albany, New York's capital. I saw some of his collection at the beautiful Rockefeller estate with sweeping views of the Hudson River in Pocantico, Westchester County. But the bulk of his huge collection is in Albany.

In the mid-1960s, Nelson Rockefeller gave a talk at the New School for Social Research, the arts-oriented adult education school in Greenwich Village, now called New School University. I was a trustee there and was delighted to have Nelson as a speaker. The auditorium was packed. Nelson was supposed to speak about the history of art for perhaps 30 to 40 minutes. After an hour and a half, his wife Happy had to cut him off. If she had not, he probably would have gone on for two or three hours. That was typical of Nelson's enthusiasm and his ability to get completely immersed in art. He was absolutely enraptured by the subject.

I was interested to discover how much he really knew about art history and how proud he was of his family's support for art, particularly his mother's. Nelson and his mother helped make contemporary art popular.

The Rockefeller collection is also represented at the Metropolitan where a primitive art wing was established to honor Nelson's son Michael, who disappeared while exploring New Guinea. Using many of the works of art that Michael collected in the South Pacific, Nelson put together this important collection with the help of Rene d'Harnoncourt and the distinguished art scholar Robert Goldwater, an editor of the art magazine published for many years by the American Federation of Arts.

I always liked Goldwater and his wife, Louise Bourgeois, a prominent sculptor whose work was featured in the May 2000 opening show of the Tate Modern in London. She was angry at me because I never bought her work. I should have bought her sculpture of Robert. I didn't because I was too tight to pay $28,000 for something that was not unique. The sculpture was cast in multiples of six. Like some of Rodin's works that were cast in multiple numbers, many collectors and institutions could own it. (The Met has a Rodin exhibit. Some of the same sculptures are at Stanford University, on the Mall in Washington, and in smaller museums around the country. They are wonderful, but no one institution or collector has something singular.)

A slew of adjectives has been used to describe Nelson Rockefeller: ebullient, intense, resilient, optimistic, quick, restless, energetic, assertive. I agree with all of those assessments. He had an easy-going boyish charm reenforced by slangy, punchy talk, and a broad smile. He was unembarrassed by his wealth and put it to good use.

Like me, Nelson was exhilarated by purchasing works of art he admired. He enjoyed the chase and the decision making as much as actually owning the work of art.

THE INCOMPARABLE JIM SOBY

James Thrall Soby, a man of great good humor and a major curator at the Museum of Modern Art (director of the Department of Painting and Sculpture), had great influence on me, perhaps second only to Duncan Phillips. I learned from discussing art with him, watching his personal collection grow, and observing what he did at MoMA.

Soby specialized in surrealist art. He was particularly interested in Italians like Giorgio de Chirico, who painted scenes of areas in Rome with shadows of walking figures. Soby had the best collection of de Chirico and did some important writing about de Chirico and the Italian Futurists.

In the early 1940s, Mt. Holyoke College asked him to loan paintings from his personal collection for an exhibition. He agreed on condition that the exhibit also include works from my collection. As a result, we put on a joint show of Jim's Europeans and my Americans. Jim was extremely knowledgeable about my collection, about his paintings, and about the art world of the time. He was also such an amusing person that the exhibit was a happy adventure.

Following the exhibit, he wrote that the Americans stood up very well to European competition. This was one of the earliest confirmations of my own positive assessment of twentieth-century American art.

After the show, I gave Mt. Holyoke six paintings: Milton Avery's *Discussion 1944*, depicting two women sitting on a couch and chatting; Louis Michel Eilshemius' *Three Girls Bathing*; Robert Henri's touching portrait, *Annie Lavelle, 1928*; John Marin's *The Harbor, 1910*; Charles Sheeler's dynamic *Horses 1946*, and Abraham Walkowitz's dramatic *Isadora Duncan*.

Jim apparently approved of my taste. After our joint show at Mt. Holyoke, he asked my help in choosing a Morris Louis painting for MoMA's permanent collection. The Guggenheim Museum was featuring an exhibition of Morris Louis' paintings, and we went to see it together. We chose a picture that MoMA bought.

Mt. Holyoke awarded me an honorary degree on a beautiful sunny day in May 1999. I don't know if I deserved it. I never got beyond the first semester of college, but I now have honorary degrees from Bar Ilan University in Israel, from Purchase College of the State University of New York, from New School University, and a Doctor of Fine Arts from Mt. Holyoke, where Jim Soby and I held our art show many years ago.

THE ARTIST'S CHAMPION: DOROTHY MILLER

No one was more important to twentieth-century American artists than MoMA curator Dorothy Miller, a key figure in developing the great collection of modern American art at MoMA. Alfred Barr brought twentieth-century art to the attention of the American public. Dorothy Miller directed that focus toward American artists. Her support of American artists in the exhibitions she mounted was crucial to establishing a number of important careers. She was far more significant, to my mind, than her reputation in the community.

You would never hear her say anything of the kind, but Dorothy Miller was the person most responsible for the developing appreciation of modern American art at MoMA and throughout the country. She was particularly important in bringing Mark Rothko to public attention.

Her involvement with American artists was important for them, for the museum, and for the public that came to appreciate homegrown modern art. Dorothy created six exhibitions featuring American artists—"Americans 1941" and five other years. She discovered artists who went on to make history, such as Rothko, William Baziotes, Clyford Still, and Irving Kriesberg. She showed Jackson Pollock early.

I acquired works by Pollock, Rothko, Kriesberg, Baziotes and others who exhibited in Dorothy Miller's shows. I grew to appreciate Loren MacIver's art, particularly *Emmett Kelly*, an insightful portrait of the great clown, in shows mounted by Dorothy Miller.

Dorothy's husband Holger Cahill headed the WPA Federal Artists Project, which provided work for Pollock, Rothko, and Willem de Kooning, among others. Holger was a true intellectual. When he gave me one of his books to read, he said, "Roy, I don't think you will understand it." He was half-right. I partially understood it.

THE ATTACK ON ALFRED BARR

One of the saddest things I have read was a published account of Marga Barr's journal entry for October 16, 1943:

It is a gray Saturday. There are no plans. A. seems listless. M. prevails on him to go to an afternoon movie. On the way home he tells her that in the morning mail he had received a letter from Mr. Clark asking him to resign.

The letter is three pages long, single spaced. The main grievance is that A. has not produced the book on modern art that Mr. Clark and Mrs. Rockefeller have ordered him to write . . .

The effect on A. is one of nausea and contempt for the obtuseness of Clark, who obviously has no understanding of the scope or purpose of the museum. M. is torn between shock and outrage at this heartless dismissal.

Incredibly, Alfred Barr, the genius behind the Modern Museum, was fired as its director. He was fired by Stephen Clark, who was president of the museum and never should have been.

Clark inherited a substantial fortune from Singer Sewing Machine and Clark Thread companies. He was important to the museum because he contributed $50,000 a year, a handsome sum in MoMA's early days.

Clark's collection, now at the Metropolitan Museum and at Yale University, focused on paintings by Matisse and other early twentieth-century artists. He was stuck in that period. By 1940 he was reactionary, not only in his personality and outlook on life but also in his collecting.

I understood his kind of collecting because in some ways, after my early period of discovery as a collector, I was something of a reactionary. I tried to use good taste in buying works that pleased me, but after a while my acquisitions weren't breakthroughs the way my earlier collecting was.

Clark became president of the museum because, as World War II loomed, Nelson Rockefeller left for Washington to become Coordinator of Inter-American Affairs in the State Department. Once we were at war, it was impossible to keep Nelson focused on the museum. Other Trustees who supported Barr, such as Philip Johnson and Eddie Warburg, were in the Army. Mrs. Rockefeller's attention at that time was centered on the recreation of a colonial village at Williamsburg, Virginia, another Rockefeller venture. Left in charge of the museum was a group of reactionaries who had little appreciation of Barr as the guiding genius.

As director, Alfred tried to do everything. He mediated every fight, arranged every show, acquired every piece of art for the permanent collection, ran the staff and the Trustees, made the speeches, and did the research and writing at which he excelled.

No one, not even Barr, could have done all that alone without sacrificing some aspect of his mission. Early in life, I learned the importance of delegating. Barr found that difficult. Compounding his heavy workload was his frail health.

Stephen Clark took advantage of Barr's known administrative shortcomings and the absence of his supporters. It is a sad story. Everyone who knew Barr found it difficult to believe that it actually happened. But it did.

In the letter from Clark that Barr received that Saturday morning in 1943, he was informed that he was no longer director, that his salary was cut in half, and that he was being moved to a corner of the library where he could do his writing.

The salary cut was especially cruel. Alfred lived so frugally that he took the Madison Avenue bus, which cost a nickel, rather than the Fifth Avenue bus, which might have been more convenient but cost ten cents.

Alfred's colleagues said, forget that he fired you, stay in your office and do your work. He did. Mr. Clark didn't pay much attention.

Alfred was a sensitive man. It was a difficult time for him. But his colleagues made it easier because they had such great admiration for him.

RENE D'HARNONCOURT

The first few years after Clark's firing of Barr were difficult for Barr and for the museum. New directors came and went. But Barr's changed role was made easier when Rene d'Harnoncourt became director. D'Harnoncourt recognized Barr's importance to MoMA and treated him with the greatest respect. Rene was an extremely tall, much beloved man who served almost twenty years as director. He had an unusual combination of talents: tremendous knowledge of art, great administrative skill, and a lot of tact and understanding.

Like Barr, he helped the Rockefellers, Whitneys, Palleys, and others in purchases for their private collections.

The d'Harnoncourts had a country home in the Hamptons on Long Island. One summer day, Rene, who was a little hard of hearing, was taking his usual morning walk down a country lane when a car ran into him and killed him. Most likely, he didn't hear the car approach. This was a terrible tragedy.

Rene's daughter Anne d'Harnoncourt is director of the Philadelphia Museum of Art. The Philadelphia is a grand museum, and she is simply wonderful. I saw her there in 1999 and she took me around. She has done a great job.

MoMA COMES TO MY HOME

In March 1944, I received a letter to warm the heart of any collector, particularly one still relatively young and untested. It came from Harry Bull, editor of *Town & Country* magazine, who was chair of the Museum of Modern Art's committee on visiting private collections. Mr. Bull asked if the group could see my paintings. He said that the committee had not been able to find a private collection in New York of similar quality.

Of course, they could come. It was a great compliment to me as a collector and a supporter of contemporary artists. The MoMA committee wanted to see my pictures because I was already considered a somewhat brave collector, willing to take a chance on new artists.

I had developed a collection of more than twenty paintings in a relatively short time. Most were the work of young, new American artists who developed into major figures in the twentieth-century art world. At the time of MoMA visit, I already had the Birnbaum and the Gropper, Peter Hurd's *Boy from the Plains*, Ben Shahn's dramatic *India*, Marsden Hartley's masterpiece, *Fishermen's Last Supper*, George L. K. Morris' *From a Church Door*, Jacob Lawrence's brilliant *Evangelists* from his Harlem series, Darrel Austin's provocative *The Legend*, Stuart Davis' stunning *Barber Shop*, Jack Levine's thought provoking *The Banquet*, Rufino Tamayo's arresting *Woman Spinning*, Ralston Crawford's striking *At the Dock*, Abraham Rattner's charming *April Showers*, which has always been a great favorite of mine, and of course, the terrific *Gaspé Landscape* by Milton Avery.

On the appointed day, I raced home from the office as soon as the stock market closed and found about 100 people at my home. Some members of MoMA committee had already come and gone. Nelson Rockefeller must have been among them because some years later, when he offered to buy my entire collection, he was quite familiar with it.

While my guests looked around, I overheard one elderly lady say, "I don't know why they wanted to see the Neuberger collection. Mine is much better." I agreed. The speaker was Adelaide Milton de Groot, who had a superb collection of European and American art. In her will she bequeathed her entire collection to the Metropolitan Museum of Art.

When Tom Hoving was director of the Met and wanted to raise money to purchase a famous Velazquez, he sold several items, including art that had been donated by Adelaide de Groot. The sale caused a great ruckus, and with good reason. (See "Hoving and the Velazquez Affair" in Chapter 7.)

Since that visit of the contributing members of the Museum of Modern Art, we have opened our home more times than I can count to visiting groups, but the thrill was in that first one.

That early visit was a vote of confidence in my collection and my judgment from a group of people and an institution I admired tremendously. It helped me develop confidence in myself.

The seal of approval from MoMA, at a time when I think my taste was getting a bit better, helped me become more adventurous.

GIFTS TO BRYN MAWR

Alfred Barr was responsible for my donating eight paintings to Bryn Mawr College. In 1946, he gave the Mary Flexner lectures at Bryn Mawr, a scholarly place with a good art department. The Flexner lecture series is quite distinguished. Barr gave his lectures in February and March and came back enthused by the Pennsylvania countryside campus.

"Roy," he said, "why don't you give Bryn Mawr some paintings? You have so many. They have a great art department but no museum. If you gave them a few paintings, it might be the beginning of a museum."

I said, "Well, Alfred, that is easy for me to do. My wife went there, so that is an extra inducement."

So, at Alfred's urging, Marie and I met with the head of the art department. We spent a couple of nights in an old house on the campus called the Deanery. This house had been the home of Bryn Mawr's first president. We stayed in a large room with a bathroom down the hall. When we went out to brush our teeth before going to bed, we noticed a glass in the bathroom with someone's teeth in it. Marie and I got the giggles and could not contain them for a good deal of the night. In the morning, the teeth were gone.

In 1948, I gave Bryn Mawr eight paintings, including a large, dramatic Milton Avery portrait of his daughter March, *Young Artist Standing*, and a Suzy Frelinghuysen, *Composition 1944*, an abstract evocative of a violin in muted colors of yellow, blue, tan, and black. It is a striking work. Suzy was a singer as well as an artist, so musical themes came naturally into her work.

I also gave Bryn Mawr a William Zorach watercolor and paintings by David Aronson, Edward Stevens, John Heliker, Raymond Breinin, and Romare Bearden.

Bryn Mawr never did establish an art museum. Today, these paintings are usually in the campus center, a nineteenth-century gymnasium that I enabled the College to renovate. They built a larger gymnasium, so this historic building could be remodeled.

Although the center is not a museum, it displays their art collection very nicely, including the eight pictures I gave them.

THE GOOD OLD MODERN

The Museum of Modern Art has gone through many leadership upheavals and weathered them all. It is now in wonderful shape, large and popular, and more important than ever.

In 1995, MoMA appointed as director Glenn Lowry, an art historian educated at Williams and Harvard. From the start, he was acclaimed for his energy, scholarship, and ability to handle the storms that besiege MoMA from time to time.

MoMA's then president, Agnes Gund, was a terrific organizer, a superb leader and a marvelous speaker. I have been told that in 1998, Agnes Gund wanted MoMA to buy a Mary Frank sculpture but the staff didn't want to spend the money. The budget had already been allocated for other purchases. Agnes then announced that she would leave a Frank sculpture to the museum in her will. When I heard that, I thought, this is a story where everyone wins. The museum will have a work Agnes wants them to have, without spending the money they didn't want to spend.

A PARTY FOR KITTY CARLISLE HART

MoMA gives splendid parties. Every spring they hold a gala in the sculpture garden. When my wife Marie was alive, this was an event she especially enjoyed.

In June 1999, they held an enormous party in honor of my great friend, Kitty Carlisle Hart. Kitty was honored for her many contributions to the arts, including twenty years as the gracious and hard-working chair of the New York State Council on the Arts, appointed by Governors Hugh Carey and Mario Cuomo. She first joined the Council as vice-chair, appointed by Governor Nelson Rockefeller.

The party was an outpouring of affection for a much-loved public servant by hundreds of people involved in the arts. In response to the toasts and applause, Kitty sang three songs, an Irving Berlin, a Richard Rodgers, and a Cole Porter. She sings splendidly.

After dinner, the guests danced among the sculptures in the garden. It was a beautiful sight but the music sounded so loud that, after just a dance or two, Kitty and I escaped to my car to go home. In our younger years, we might have danced till dawn.

Roy Neuberger and David Rockefeller, La Guardia Dinner, New York Hilton, 1982. (Photo by Karen Zebulon.)

CHAPTER SIX

THE COLLECTORS

Just as artists and writers benefit each other, so do collectors. Getting to know other collectors has been a splendid side-benefit of collecting art.

This may not be typical, but I don't feel a sense of rivalry toward other collectors or a feeling of regret that I don't have certain paintings that they do. I have looked at other people's collections as I would look in a museum or a gallery. Often it is an education.

I have been told that some collectors look closely at my collection. I am happy that some have followed in the direction that I charted.

THE INCOMPARABLE DUNCAN PHILLIPS

I mentioned my first visit to the Phillips Gallery (now the Phillips Collection) in Washington, about eight months after my return from Paris in 1929, when I first met Duncan Phillips, the gallery's founder, a lovely man with courtly manners who would become the strongest influence on my collecting career. I told him that I wanted to be a collector. Although I was clearly a young man of modest means, he was very attentive to me—quite a different reception from the one I had from Alfred Stieglitz, who threw me out of his gallery.

The Phillips Collection already included Renoir's *Luncheon of the Boating Party*, Daumier's *Uprising*, as well as the finest paintings by Cezanne, Bonnard, and Monet, and works by contemporary Americans.

Every piece at the Phillips was carefully selected. The gallery showed the best work of each artist.

Duncan was born in 1886 in Pittsburgh. The family moved to Washington near DuPont Circle. In 1921, they invited the public into their home to view their art collection. They showed paintings by French Impressionists such as Monet and Sisley, but they also featured American artists, among them Whistler, Davies, Twachtman, and Hassam. The Phillips home gradually developed into the Phillips Gallery.

Thirty-seven years after our first meeting, at a small Sunday morning gathering in Washington, a now frail Duncan Phillips told me, "You are the only one whose taste resembles mine. I would like to see you have a museum in New York like mine in Washington." I was elated at this judgment of my collection and I looked forward to our future conversations about such a project.

Sadly, Duncan Phillips died just a few months later. But he had planted the seed for what would become the Neuberger Museum of Art.

In 1999, the Phillips Collection paid tribute to its founder with a show called *Renoir to Rothko: The Eye of Duncan Phillips*, featuring 361 works collected by Phillips, displayed in both the old Phillips mansion and the newer annex. Long lines of people waited to gain entrance. Once inside, they stayed. The tiny lunchroom, normally a quiet corner in the basement of the mansion, was jammed all day: Visitors didn't want to leave the museum, even for a sandwich. It would have pleased Duncan Phillips to know that younger generations appreciate and value his taste.

SAM AND MARGARET LEWISOHN

Van Gogh's *L'Arlesienne* hung in the dining room and Picassos were all over the place at Sam and Margaret Lewisohn's home on Manhattan's East Side. I loved going to parties there in the 1940s. Margaret, one of the great people of the world, provided a setting that was always fun. I liked her enormously.

At the Lewisohns, I met other admirers of their collection, including the publisher George Delacorte, the actress Helen Hayes, Oscar Hammerstein's wife Dorothy, Mrs. Little Hull (the second wife of Vincent Astor), the lawyer Morton Baum, who played the piano beautifully, and Newbold Morris, brother of the artist George L. K. Morris and descendant of Gouverneur Morris, a signer of the Declaration of Independence. Newbold ran for mayor but he never made it. He became an excellent Commissioner of Parks. He was an extremely nice man. His brother George was equally nice and he was brilliant.

It was said that the Lewisohns opened their home to more than 3,000 art lovers a year. I believe it.

Margaret Seligman Lewisohn was an accomplished musician, a founder of Bennington College, and one of New York's great hostesses. She knew Sam when he made his first art purchase, a Georges Seurat drawing, at the age of nineteen. Sam wrote in his book, *Painters and Personality* (1937, Harper & Bros.), that he selected paintings that reflected the artist's personality. He considered abstract compositions and their creators to be immature. In some cases, maybe he was right, but his verdict was far too sweeping.

You can get a sense of Sam's taste at the Metropolitan Museum, which now has most of his collection. He did not have a huge amount of art, but the quality was first rate.

He gave the Met an oil sketch for Seurat's *Sunday on La Grande Jatte-1884*, the famous painting of Parisians at leisure on a summer weekend on an island in the Seine. It is an exact replica in miniature of the large final painting that is about 7 feet by 10 feet and occupies an entire wall at the Art Institute of Chicago.

I doubt that the large painting will ever again be seen anywhere but in Chicago. On loan to MoMA, the pointillist masterpiece was almost destroyed in a fire. The Art Institute of Chicago said they would never again lend it.

La Grande Jatte is an unbelievable picture, the best example of the pointillist movement, and may well be the best painting of the nineteenth century.

The Jeu de Paumes in Paris (where the Impressionists were exhibited before the opening of the vast Impressionist space at the Musee D'Orsay) had only one Seurat, donated by the early twentieth-century American collector John Quinn. A Seurat of the quality of the Lewisohn gift was a great coup for the Met.

Sam was a wealthy man from one of New York's most prominent families. Although his gift to the Metropolitan Museum was smaller than that of the Havemeyers or Annenbergs, it was commensurate in quality. If a person has one fantastic painting, I'd say that is a great collector.

In 1951, I met Sam Lewisohn at a Rufino Tamayo show at the Knoedler Gallery in New York. "I'm so happy," he said. "I have always wanted to own a Tamayo, and I bought one, a really fine one."

A few days later he went to visit his friend Edward G. Robinson, the actor and Impressionist collector, in Santa Barbara, California. Sam died there of a heart attack.

I sometimes think of Sam when I view Tamayo's *Woman Spinning*, a work of great strength, on my living room wall at home. I understood Sam's excitement. I felt the same way when I bought *Woman Spinning* from Val Dudensing at the Valentine Gallery in 1943. I don't want to part with it, but I have loaned it to shows all over the country.

Margaret Lewisohn served on the Board of Trustees of Vassar College. In June 1954, she drove Illinois Governor Adlai Stevenson, who had been the Democratic candidate for president in 1952, to Poughkeepsie where he delivered the Commencement address at Vassar. On the way back she dropped Governor Stevenson in Westchester and continued home. She never got there. A terrible accident occurred on one of the sharp curves on the Taconic Parkway. She was killed. I was shocked when I learned of her death. If she had lived longer, Margaret would have been even more outstanding in making our civilization a little better.

As I have said, I have no love for the automobile. I have known too many people who were killed in car accidents—my wife Marie's younger brother, the sculptor David Smith, MoMA director Rene d'Harnoncourt, Jackson Pollock, and Margaret Lewisohn. They all had much more to contribute to the world when their lives were cut short.

ROBERT LEHMAN

Robert Lehman was born to be a collector. His father Philip, who created the original Lehman Brothers investment banking house (later Shearson Lehman), was a distinguished collector who concentrated on old masters and drawings. Young Bobby inherited his father's interest in art. While still at Yale he was already involved in both art and finance. He added significantly to the great art collection he inherited.

Lehman was a dual character, a powerful leader of Lehman Brothers, one of the most important banking institutions, and a collector equal to any in the world. He was both a Trustee and a vice president of the Metropolitan Museum. I always thought that he aspired to be president of the museum, something that never happened.

After Bobby Lehman died, Lehman Brothers came under the direction of new managers who couldn't get along with one another. While he was alive, Bobby Lehman kept it together without any problem.

Bobby Lehman left a lot of art to the Metropolitan Museum—nearly 2,000 individual items—drawings, which are the heart of the collection, as well as paintings, sculpture, and a group of unusual frames. He did not collect much nineteenth- or twentieth-century art. The main strengths of the Lehman collection are its old masters drawings.

The bequest had many strings attached, many tough restrictions. It called for a new wing to house the collection, which caused one of the major controversies during the tempestuous years from 1967 to 1977 when Thomas Hoving was director of the Met. The proposed Lehman Wing was controversial because it would intrude a little into Central Park. Many New Yorkers opposed the Met's taking over any more park land. But the Metropolitan building, constructed in the 1870s and 1880s, left no room for the future. The Met's collections had grown enormously. There was no place to put them.

John Lindsay was mayor at the time, and Tom Hoving, who had served as Lindsay's parks commissioner, asked me to go down to City Hall to help seek approval for the new wing. I went with some other Trustees. It took a number of hearings before we finally got New York City approval.

And that's that, I think, as far as any more expansion is concerned. The Met now includes the new American Wing, the Egyptian Temple of Dendur, the Primitive Art Wing—and the Lehman Wing, a useful addition for showing exhibitions appropriate to its architecture as well as housing the superb Lehman collection.

Lehman's bequest was controversial in another way. He wanted the new wing to contain a replica of his Fifty-fourth Street home. Ultimately, it was decided to replicate only a part of the Lehman home.

If this were Paris, the collection would have been left in the Lehman Fifty-fourth Street town house. The Louvre, for example, has several buildings that are part of the museum. The Met has the Cloisters in upper Manhattan where medieval art is exhibited. There is plenty of precedent for a museum showing works of art elsewhere than in its main building.

Why did the Met give the Lehman collection so much space? Part of the answer lies in the nature of museum directors and curators. A director has a few things he wants to accomplish while at the head of an institution. First, he wants to collect, and, when possible, collect something spectacular. If in one fell swoop he can acquire objects reputed to be worth $100 million or so, it isn't something to pass up. Directors also want to show collections in the best possible settings. Often that involves adding to the space of the museum.

It is in the basic nature of museums that directors keep acquiring more objects, and needing more display space. This was especially true of Tom Hoving, who I think wanted to go down in history as the greatest museum director of all time.

EDWARD ROOT

One of the great collectors of Hopper was Edward Root, son of New York Senator Elihu Root, who in 1919 got tariffs removed from imported art, thus allowing Americans to collect European art. Senator Root earlier had been Teddy Roosevelt's Secretary of State and in 1909 founded the American Federation of Arts.

The Senator's son Edward was a rather subdued, scholarly resident of Clinton, New York, an upstate community near Hamilton College. He was much older than me and had acquired a significant amount of twentieth-century American abstract art. Root was a respectable, professorial, comparatively wealthy man, so respectable that he bought more judiciously than I did. Everyone starts a bit conservative, too conservative. Then you have to take some risks. Although I was somewhat more adventurous than Root, I admired him a great deal.

Root had excellent taste and bought beautiful works. His collection was at least equal to mine, and many of the art objects were better. He particularly liked Hopper, Demuth, and Feininger. Edward Root specialized in American art and seemed to have acquired it for the same reason I did: for love of the picture, the composition, the color. He was closer to my kind of collecting than anyone else in the country, but he didn't exhibit his beautiful collection. I saw it in his home. Nonetheless, it was a pleasure to find another collector who believed that living artists were producing great art.

JOSEPH HIRSHHORN

Joe Hirshhorn came to the United States as a youngster and went to work as an office boy on Wall Street when he was fourteen years old. By the time he was seventeen, he was a millionaire.

In 1929, just before the October Panic, he took all his money to Canada where he got involved in mining uranium. He came back with a huge fortune—a check for $49.5 million from the Rio Tinto Mines.

Hirshhorn became one of the most inventive collectors, particularly of sculpture. He loved Rodin. Perhaps his greatest purchase was Rodin's *The Burghers of Calais*, a large and important sculpture now placed prominently at the Hirshhorn Museum.

Personally, I'm skeptical about what a lot of museums are doing today, acquiring what I call reproductions, castings of sculptures made long after Rodin died. Museums accepted these later Rodin castings from Iris and B. G. Cantor, who are major donors to the Metropolitan Museum. I could be wrong but I think that taking an old casting of a Henry Moore sculpture long after he died is not the same as buying a Henry Moore sculpture while he was alive.

Joe Hirshhorn and I saw each other in the 1940s and 1950s at New York galleries. At that time, we were reputed to be the two largest collectors. In fact, he had much more art than I did, but he did not share my passion for helping to support living artists. However, like me, he bought a number of artists early in their career.

Abram Lerner, a knowledgeable man of dignity and quality, became Joe's advisor. I knew Lerner fairly well and thought highly of him. Lerner might gather the paintings or sculptures to select from, but Joe made the selections himself. In the early days, it was likely to be sculpture. After Hirshhorn died in 1981, Lerner became director of the Hirshhorn Museum.

When Nelson Rockefeller was governor of New York, he asked Joe Hirshhorn, whose collection was a good bit larger than mine, to donate it to New York State. Governor Rockefeller might have made a deal for a museum on the State University's Purchase campus with Hirshhorn rather than with me.

Joe parlayed the Rockefeller offer for a museum built by New York State into a museum in Washington, DC. He got President Lyndon Johnson and the federal government to build the Joseph H. Hirshhorn Museum and Sculpture Garden on the Mall as part of the Smithsonian. President Johnson said that acquiring that collection was a great coup. Some question whether the museum belongs on the Mall with the Washington and Lincoln memorials.

For the opening of the Hirshhorn Museum, Joe bought a lot of paintings in a hurry. He had the money to make up for lost time. He put together a world-class collection, particularly strong in nineteenth- and twentieth-century sculpture and modern American painting, and donated it to the U.S. government. It took fifty-five trucks to cart the collection to Washington.

I sat at Joe's table at the opening of the Hirshhorn Museum in October 1974, six months after the Neuberger Museum of Art opened in Purchase, New York. Whatever Joe's shortcomings, they were not in his judgment about collecting. He was one of the great collectors.

TEXAS COLLECTORS: IMA HOGG AND ROBERT STRAUS

After World War II, collecting spread all over the country. It was no longer an Eastern establishment thing.

While I was president of the American Federation of Arts, I went twice to Texas, in 1957 to Houston and in 1963 to Dallas-Fort Worth, where I got to know two Texas collectors.

Culturally, Houston was extremely backward in 1957. The AFA meeting marked the emergence of a new cultural interest, making the city a livelier place.

One truly cultivated Texan was Ima Hogg, the daughter of a Texas governor. You've heard the old jokes about Ima Hogg and her sister Ura. There was no Ura Hogg, but Ima Hogg was a real and very sophisticated person. Her home, filled with art, including a fine Picasso, was an oasis in the city of Houston. The other oasis was Robert Straus, not the Democratic political leader but a man whose family went into the saddlery business right after the Civil War. It grew into a large company. Straus came to see me in New York in 1943 and we became friends.

Straus originally collected porcelains and oriental art. After visiting me, he switched to contemporary art and became a large collector. Much of the collection was in his home, an estate right in the middle of Houston where he lived with his wife and five children. He and his family greatly enhanced my stay in Houston.

He sold the home after the children were grown. His son, who stops by my office to this day, was highly critical of his father for the move. The son had advised keeping the house and its grounds as a real estate investment. It was good advice.

J. PAUL GETTY AND THE GETTY MUSEUM

J. Paul Getty had more money than the Rockefellers. The Getty Museum, rising high above Los Angeles on 110 acres of prime real estate, cost over $1 billion to build. The art it houses was bought in the late twentieth century with the great Getty oil fortune. The Getty Foundation has over $6 billion. They are rich enough to outbid almost anybody for anything that comes on the market, but they can't buy a collection like that of the Metropolitan. An individual collector might sell a work or two to the Getty, but the Metropolitan is not about to sell any of its masterpieces.

There is a great dearth of twentieth-century art at the Getty. They don't have much late nineteenth-century art either. The collection stops with a few Impressionists in a small room. Here is this great post-modern collection of buildings comprising the museum, state of the art late 1990s, but inside the museum the twentieth century doesn't exist.

However, the Getty Museum sponsors a great deal of valuable research. And the museum has retained the wonderful old Getty Museum of ancient art in Malibu.

ART IN KANSAS CITY: WILLIAM NELSON AND LAURENCE SICKMAN

In 1952, I went to Asia where I saw some marvelous ancient art at the museum in Taiwan, but I got very little feeling from it. It didn't do much for me.

To see great Chinese art, I prefer the Metropolitan Museum in New York and the William Rockhill Nelson Gallery at the Nelson-Atkins Museum of Art in Kansas City, Missouri, a huge museum second in size in America to the Metropolitan Museum of Art. I recommend a trip to Kansas City if only to visit the museum.

The Kansas City story began in 1880 when William Nelson, a young journalist, arrived in town and proceeded to build the *Kansas City Star* into an important and very successful newspaper. He made a lot of money and wanted to do something for the city in which he took pride. Although not an art collector himself, Nelson thought

Kansas City should have a significant art museum. In his will, he left funds to build a large museum with an impressive sculpture hall boasting columns of black marble imported from the Pyrenees.

The museum was built in the early 1930s, at a time when money went a long way. Laurence Sickman, an expert on Chinese art and a highly respected leader in the art world, became director. Sickman was a contemporary of Francis Henry Taylor of the Met, though he lived much longer than Taylor did. Although Sickman did not collect for himself, I consider him a great collector because he virtually transformed the art scene in Kansas City. With Nelson's money, he was able to buy a huge amount of Chinese art during the Depression. The extensive Asian collection is unique. He also bought paintings by Titian, El Greco, the Impressionists, and other great artists, including a lot of good American art.

When Sickman was at my home in 1977, following his honorary degree ceremony at Columbia University, he fondled the one piece of Chinese art I own and declared it to be a comparative masterpiece. He asked if I would let the Nelson Gallery have it. I was too fond of it to let it go. It is a prize piece in my apartment. Ultimately, it goes to the Neuberger Museum, which will then have one Chinese piece, but a great one.

Mark Wilson, chosen by Sickman as his successor, was the director when I visited Kansas City. Wilson is one of a number of extraordinary directors in recent years. The talent in the art world today is breathtaking.

MARIE AND AVERELL HARRIMAN

I have judged shows in a number of museums, among them the Walker Art Center in Minneapolis and the Butler Museum in Youngstown, Ohio. On several occasions I judged an art show held in Gramercy Park to award the Wolfe Prize, which recognizes outstanding women artists. The Metropolitan Museum was interested in Mrs. Catharine Lorillard Wolfe, sponsor of the prize and a friend of Marie Harriman. Once I judged the show with Lloyd Goodrich of the Whitney. Another time I judged it with Marie Harriman, whose husband Averell was then governor of New York. She invited my wife Marie and me for dinner. The Harrimans lived around the corner from us, on East Eighty-first Street between Fifth and Madison Avenues, in a townhouse filled with art.

Marie Harriman was both an art collector and for a time, a dealer with an attractive gallery on Madison Avenue. Most of the day-to-day work in the gallery was done by the lovely, cultured Ann Sardi, whose brother Vincent, a Columbia College graduate, owned *Sardi's*, the celebrated restaurant in the theatrical district.

The death of Marie Harriman, in 1977, was a blow not only to her family and friends but to the world of art.

HOWARD AND JEAN LIPMAN

I covered the walls of my office, reception rooms, hallways, and the offices of my partners and associates with contemporary paintings, encouraging my colleagues at Neuberger & Berman to become collectors themselves.

Howard Lipman, one of my partners, and his wife, Jean, needed little encouragement. As collectors, they were as good as they come. Beginning in the 1930s, Jean edited the magazine *Art in America*, which Howard owned. Howard was a sculptor in his free time. In my country home, I have a sculpture of a hippopotamus done by Howard that is really pretty good. Before he came to Wall Street, he had been a milliner, making hats with his aunt.

The Lipmans were early collectors. At their house in Cannondale, Connecticut, they collected American primitive art and sculptures by David Smith, Louise Nevelson, and Sandy Calder whose biography the Lipmans wrote.

AUCTIONS

Many collectors or their representatives spend a great deal of time at auctions. I was infrequently at auctions but I remember two in particular.

I went to one because I was interested in a painting by Andrew Wyeth. Aline Bernstein (later Aline Saarinen, wife of the renowned architect Eero Saarinen) urged me to buy it. Aline's judgment was good. She wrote one of the best books about collectors, *The Proud Possessors* (Random House, 1958). In the 1950s, she was associate art critic of *The New York Times.*

It was a rare moment, the only time when a Wyeth was up for auction. And it was well within my means. But my wife Marie did not like it.

Both these women were with me at the auction. I had one lady on one side telling me to bid and the other lady on the other side, saying, "Don't bid," and I had great respect for them both. I listened to Marie. She rarely interfered with my acquiring art. The Wyeth and the early James Brooks were the only pictures that she restrained me from buying.

I went with Marie and Aline to another auction. Mary Sullivan, the MoMA cofounder who became a dealer after her husband's losses in the 1929 panic, had to sell their marvelous collection of paintings. The auction was held in the Parke-Bernet Galleries on December 6, 1939, while we were still deep in the Depression.

My strongest memory of that evening is what I didn't do. One of the paintings offered was a major Maurice Prendergast oil, *The Bathers* painted in 1912—a year before the Armory show that introduced modern painting to America. I liked the painting, and I could have had it for $500. Of course, $500 at that moment was a fairly large amount.

I didn't buy it. At that time I was only buying works by living artists. I hesitated to buy a picture by Maurice Prendergast, who had died in 1924.

Twenty years later, in 1959, Prendergast's *The Bathers* was again on the market. I admired it enough so that I bought it for $9,000 from Harold Milch, an independent dealer whose father owned the Milch Gallery. The painting is now at the Neuberger Museum.

In 1956, I had purchased a small Prendergast watercolor, *Spanish Steps, Rome*, from the Kraushaar Gallery. It is a lovely depiction of the Roman landmark in 1898 or 1899. The painting shows people climbing up and down the glorious Spanish Steps. Usually, oil paintings are more valuable than watercolors. But the Prendergast unfinished watercolor *Spanish Steps* was more valuable than many oils. It is one of Prendergast's most popular works.

Several artists liked to work in watercolor. John Marin went in that direction even more than Prendergast. I have three John Marin watercolors, all bought while he was alive. My favorite is *The Harbor 1910* which I acquired in 1953 and particularly like because it is the Manhattan waterfront. Its abstract aura conveys the energy of my city, my Wall Street.

A watercolor is done more quickly than an oil. I particularly like Marin's dry brush technique in watercolor, akin to a work in oil. His shorthand depiction of nature is a marvel of structure.

THE COLLECTORS CLUB

At the American Federation of Arts, where I served as president for twenty years, we created the Collectors Club of America. There were a few single men and women in the club, but basically it was a hundred couples. After the membership was formed, no one could get in unless a vacancy was created when somebody moved or died.

Two people helped me create the club—George Fitch, who soon after left the East Coast, and Eloise Spaeth, a minor collector but a major character in the art world. She and her husband Otto, who was fairly well-to-do, moved from Dayton, Ohio, to a gorgeous apartment in the East Sixties, near my home. Eloise wrote several books about art and art galleries. Anyone interested in what was happening in the museums and art galleries in the 1960s should take a look at her excellent guides.

The Collectors Club raised money for AFA. Membership cost $250 a year. A hundred people, $250 a year. In those days it was a lot of money.

Through the 1950s and early 1960s, the Collectors Club gathered at formal dinners held in various museums, such as the Guggenheim. After Francis Taylor left as director of the Met and returned to Worcester, Massachusetts, where he started, we went to hear him talk and to visit the Worcester Art Museum.

One meeting was at the Brooklyn Museum. I had already changed my perspective of only buying works by living artists. That evening at the Brooklyn pushed me another step toward becoming a collector of ancient art. Brooklyn's curator of Egyptian art, John Cooney, was a friend who became my early tutor in ancient art. He was primarily responsible for the Brooklyn Museum's great acquisitions of Egyptian art. Later, he went to Cleveland and worked for Sherman Lee, the director of the Cleveland Museum of Art.

I always loved ancient art but I didn't collect it until after 1958 when I recognized that the lot of living artists had been greatly improved.

TOM HOVING ON COLLECTORS

Six years after he left the Metropolitan Museum of Art, Thomas Hoving published an article listing who, in his judgment, were the 100 greatest collectors of the twentieth century (*Connoisseur*, September 1983). The listing appeared in the handsome, now defunct *Connoisseur* magazine, which was masterminded for several years by Hoving.

Tom did a good job compiling his list. It was not just an evaluation of the moment, it was for the whole century. He did not focus only on collectors of modern art or of living artists. He included all collectors.

Hoving ranks me as number 72, just after Nelson Rockefeller, who had much more art than I did. Jim Soby, whose collection I admired enormously, is listed as 74. The great early twentieth-century collector John Quinn, who helped support James Joyce and whose handwritten manuscript of a chapter from Joyce's *Ulysses* was auctioned in December 2000, is rated as 75.

Tom Hoving's first place goes to the Mellon family, who created the National Gallery of Art in Washington. They were more than a family, they were an institution and they created one of our great institutions. Second and third were John D. and Abigail Rockefeller—she, of course, created MoMA with begrudging help from John D.—and Gertrude Stein and her family, particularly her brother Leo, for their collection of early twentieth-century art including Matisse and Picasso, especially his famous portrait of Gertrude Stein, now at the Met.

Tom gives fourth place to William Walters and Henry Walters, father and son of the nineteenth and early twentieth century whose collection forms the backbone of the Walters Art Gallery in Baltimore. They *were* important, but I wouldn't put them quite so high.

Next on the Hoving list are collectors whom I would rank higher than Hoving's number 5, the Havemeyers. H. O. Havemeyer died relatively young. His wife Louisine was more responsible for the collection than her husband. She bought European art, particularly Degas, with the encouragement of her friend, the American painter Mary Cassatt. The enormous Havemeyer collection at the Metropolitan Museum, almost 2,000 works of art, is arguably the Met's most important donation. In addition to fine Impressionists, the Havemeyers gave the Met El Greco's *View of Toledo*, Goya's *Majas on a Balcony*, and Asian and Near Eastern Art.

Henry Clay Frick is rated number 6. I would move him higher also. The Frick Collection is extraordinary. He should come after the Mellons; I would judge him number 2 and the Havemeyers number 3.

Norton Simon, rated number 7, is one of the greatest collectors in American history. I knew him when I lived in Paris in the 1920s. His collection, at the Norton Simon Museum in Pasadena, California, is nothing less than fantastic.

Isabella Stewart Gardner, ranked number 8, is one of the immortals, the founder of the Gardner Museum in Boston. She financed Bernard Berenson and was advised by him.

Henry Francis du Pont (number 9), founder of the living museum at Winterthur in Delaware, and Henry Plumer McIlhenny, the Philadelphia collector of French art, round out Hoving's first ten collectors. (See Table 6.1 for a comparison of Hoving's list versus my recommendations.)

The actor Edward G. Robinson (number 11) bought Impressionists very well. Lessing Rosenwald (number 12) is a successful collector of prints and drawings. Duncan Phillips is rated number 13. I would most certainly put him higher.

Hoving rates J. Pierpont Morgan as number 14, much lower than John D. Rockefeller. That's because Morgan bought other people's

Table 6.1 Top Ten Collectors

Tom Hoving's List	*Roy Neuberger's List*
1. The Mellon Family	1. The Mellon Family
2. John D. Jr. and Abby Rockefeller	2. Henry Clay Frick
3. Gertrude Stein Family	3. H. O. and Louisine Havemeyer
4. William and Henry Walters	4. Albert Barnes
5. H. O. and Louisine Havemeyer	5. John D. Jr. and Abby Rockefeller
6. Henry Clay Frick	6. Gertrude Stein Family
7. Norton Simon	7. William and Henry Walters
8. Isabella Stewart Gardner	8. Duncan Phillips
9. Henry Francis du Pont	9. Norton Simon
10. Henry Plumer McIlhenny	10. Isabella Stewart Gardner

collections in their entirety. He accumulated art the way he did money, wholesale amassing rather than discriminating selection. The Morgan holdings were extensive, but did not represent a personal view or sensibility. So I think Hoving got him about right.

Others who went in for quantity in a big way were the banker Jules Bache (number 15) who gave old masters to the Metropolitan, and Samuel Kress (number 16), founder of the Kresge stores which metamorphosed into Kmart. Kress was a donor to many different institutions, but did not have a collection of the quality of, for instance, Bobby Lehman.

Bobby Lehman is rated by Hoving as number 20. I would put him higher.

Ima Hogg (number 19), a lovely person, was far and away the best collector in Texas.

Next on Hoving's list are Thomas Gilcrease of Oklahoma, sometimes called an oil baron, a specialist in Indian art; Leonard Hanna Jr. a major patron of the Cleveland museum; and Charles Freer whose collection of Asian art is at the Freer Gallery, part of the Smithsonian in Washington.

Benjamin Altman (number 24) was the founder of the B. Altman & Company department store where I worked as a young man. He died in 1913 when I was ten so I had no opportunity to know him. I did know his nephew, Michael Friedsam (number 29) who headed B. Altman when I worked there. He divided his collection between the Metropolitan and the Brooklyn Museum, where my first donations went.

Avery Brundage of San Francisco is rated number 26 for his great Asian art collection. Two sisters, Dr. Claribel Cone and Etta Cone of Baltimore are given number 27. Maxim Karolik is number 31. Karolik was a Russian singer who collected nineteenth-century American art. His donations were the backbone of the Boston Museum of Fine Arts.

My friend Sam Lewisohn is rated number 32. Walter Annenberg, whose collection is prominently displayed at the Met, is number 35.

When Tom Hoving was about to leave the Met, a proposal was floated to establish an Annenberg Research Institute of Art at the Met with Hoving at its head. Fortunately, Annenberg thought better of the idea. It would have been a catastrophe. Can you imagine Philippe de Montebello having his predecessor on the premises? It wouldn't have worked.

In the spring of 2000, Kitty Carlisle Hart asked me to contribute to one of Annenberg's educational projects. I surprised her by giving more money than I should have.

Hoving ranks my friend "Shorty" Knox, the Buffalo investment banker who was a major contributor to the Albright-Knox Art Gallery in Buffalo, at number 40.

Despite his huge collection and the location of the Hirshhorn Museum on the Mall in Washington, Joseph Hirshhorn is rated number 45. Stephen Clark was rather a reactionary when he was active at the Modern Museum. Even so, Hoving rates Clark too low, number 52. Clark should not have fired Alfred Barr as director of the Modern Museum, but his collection is excellent.

Walter Arensberg, who bought the famous Duchamp painting *Nude Descending the Staircase*, which caused a flurry of controversy when it was exhibited in the 1913 Armory Show, is rated number 59. The Arensbergs were fine collectors.

It is ridiculous to rate Dr. Albert Barnes number 78. He should be in the first ten. I put him in a class with Mellon. Tom Hoving has great abilities and knows a lot, but the quality of the art exhibited at Albert Barnes' home in Merion, Pennsylvania, makes it worth the effort to see it. It is sometimes hard to arrange to visit the Barnes collection. What good is great art if you can't see it? But in recent years, the Barnes Trustees have worked to make the collection more accessible.

Walter Cummings Baker (number 83) collected drawings and antique bronzes that I first saw at his home. Much of it is now at the Metropolitan. Baker was a vice president of the Met and voted against appointing Thomas Hoving as director. Hoving got wind of it. When Baker died in 1971, most of his money, $9 million, went to Union College in upstate New York rather than to the Met.

Janos Scholz (number 85) was a lovely man and a fantastic collector, particularly of drawings, as well as being an extraordinary cellist.

I remember vividly when Emily and Burton Tremaine (number 93) bought Jasper Johns paintings. They bought his works and I didn't. I made a mistake in not collecting him.

Jasper Johns is a charming man. I spent an evening with him when the Neuberger Museum had a show of his friend Marisol's work in 2001 and I liked him a lot. He was influenced by early American art when American flags were used in a common place way.

The Tremaines sold a well-known Jasper Johns flag painting to the Whitney Museum for $1 million. They thought it was a joke that they could get $1 million for something that had cost them $800. That changed the market enormously. After that Jasper Johns became merchandise.

Victor and Sallie Ganz should be rated higher than number 99. As a young jewelry manufacturer, Victor became convinced that Picasso would prove to be the most important artist of the century. He was my customer and told me to sell his stocks so he could buy Picassos, which he thought would be more valuable than stock. He was right.

He died early in the 1980s. Some of his art was sold at auction then and the remainder after Sallie died. The two auctions raised more than $150 million.

Tom Hoving threw in a bonus on his list, bestowing number 101 on J. Paul Getty, who during his lifetime bought a lot of antiques, but the quality was not the best. Although Getty apparently knew how to make money, with rare exceptions, the Getty Museum building is better than the art it contains.

Neuberger and Portrait of Roy Neuberger by Will Barnet. (Photo by Myles Aronowitz.)

CHAPTER SEVEN

MY LOVE AFFAIR WITH THE METROPOLITAN

The Metropolitan Museum of Art has long been my haven, my passion, my great love. I have been active at the Met longer than any other living person. I don't regret a minute of it.

When I returned from Paris in 1929, the Met became my substitute for the Louvre, where I had gone two or three times a week, probably the world's second finest museum. The Uffizi in Florence, the National Gallery in London, the Prado in Madrid, and the Hermitage in St. Petersburg are also wonderful museums. But splendid as the Louvre and other European museums are, I rate the Met higher. In my view, the Metropolitan is simply the greatest museum in the world. The depth of its collections is unmatched.

The Metropolitan is divided into seventeen curatorial departments with a staff of about 2,000. It boasts, quite rightly, that it contains every category of art, in every known medium, from every part of the world, during every epoch of recorded time. The Met holds 5,000 years of art, a vast encyclopedia of civilization and culture.

For thirty-three years my family and I lived on the eighth floor of 993 Fifth Avenue, between Eightieth and Eighty-first Streets, right across the street from the Metropolitan. We enjoyed entertaining visiting artists and museum people. When James Rorimer was director of the Met, he often came across the street for a chat. So did Tom Hoving in his early days as director.

I made it possible for the Met to buy a small apartment on the second floor in our building, which became a comfortable place for people at the Met to greet artists and patrons of the arts. In all these close-by locales on Fifth Avenue—the Met, the small apartment, and my home—I came to know the directors and curators of the great Metropolitan.

FRANCIS HENRY TAYLOR (1940–1955)

During my seven decades of activity at the Met, the Museum has had four directors. The first, Francis Henry Taylor, was a stimulating character who taught me a lot.

It was sometimes said that Taylor had no feeling for the contemporary artist. I don't believe that was the case. Taylor wrote a wonderful book called *Fifty Centuries of Art* (Harper, 1954). That was his view of the Met, the chronicler of fifty centuries of civilization. The twentieth century is only one-fiftieth of it.

Taylor was the poor man's Medici, a patron of the arts though not a man of wealth himself. He was a powerful person of his time, a big man with a head crammed with information and opinions, and a man of strong character.

Taylor was the beginning of the new Met, the first person of sophistication and scholarship to head a great museum. The best museum directors are scholars. He was one of the earliest scholar-directors.

Before coming to the Met, he had been curator of medieval art at the Philadelphia Museum of Art and then director of the Worchester Art Museum in Massachusetts. When he left the Met and returned to Worchester, I visited him, and he was a gracious and highly informative host.

Taylor was famous in his time, but he is quite forgotten now.

ROBERT BEVERLY HALE (1949–1966)

I had respect bordering on reverence for Robert Beverly Hale, the Metropolitan's extraordinary curator of American art. Hale was from an aristocratic family that dated back to the American Revolution. His grandfather was the minister and author Edward Everett Hale and his cousin was novelist John P. Marquand. He taught draftsmanship and drawing at the Art Students League and I think this contact with artists sharpened his judgment. He was an artist himself and an expert on anatomy. His collecting was always interesting.

Hale ran into trouble because the Met's reactionary acquisition committee had little interest in abstract art. In the 1950s, a really modern work of art couldn't get through that committee. For instance, a painting like the abstract Resnick that hangs in my office might not have made it.

After I discovered that a donation of cash to buy a particular work was more likely to be accepted than the actual work itself, I enabled Hale to acquire the first work to be owned by the Met by Hans

Hofmann, the great teacher who strongly affected the development of abstract expressionism. I also assisted in Hale's acquisition of a beautiful George L. K. Morris painting, a Milton Avery, a Max Weber, and quite a few other works by contemporary artists.

In 1956, I encouraged Hale to buy Jackson Pollock's *Autumn Rhythm* for $30,000 . It was audacious for a museum like the Met to have bought Pollock at that time. For many it was too new, too modern. It turned out to be the last year of Pollock's life.

JAMES RORIMER (1955–1962)

James Rorimer, a medieval scholar who succeeded Taylor, often came across the street to my apartment to chat about art and about developments at the Met. It was Rorimer who discovered and advanced Tom Hoving. He also wrote a number of fascinating books, including *Survival: The Salvage and Protection of Art in War* (Abelard Press, 1950) about the operation he directed that recovered art stolen by the Nazis.

Six months before he died in 1962, Rorimer offered to name the American Wing after me if I would give the Met my collection. But the American Wing covers the nineteenth as well as the twentieth century, and includes decorative arts such as furniture and silver. Those aren't my interests and are not reflected in my collection, so I don't think it would have been a good idea, even if Rorimer had lived to pursue it. Rorimer's offer, while flattering, was highly unsophisticated. My collection is not really well-related to the American Wing, which is largely historical.

America in the nineteenth century was noted more for building railroads and other business exploits than for art. Because we were a young nation, we had to play cultural catch-up with Europe. We did have some good nineteenth-century artists whose work can now be seen in the Met's American Wing. Thomas Cole was a great landscape painter, as was Albert Bierstadt. Thomas Moran did wonderful paintings of the West. Some of the primitive artists whose works appeared to be awkward, and were available for as little as a dollar, are now highly esteemed.

Apart from a couple of James Quidors and some works by Thomas Cole, I bought very little nineteenth-century art. I did acquire a great many Eilshemius paintings from the nineteenth century that I think are quite good. But I was not really a collector of nineteenth-century art.

James Rorimer's death was painful to all of us who knew and admired him, but it was not a surprise. For many months, he had shown sad symptoms of his physical decline.

THE HOVING YEARS (1967–1977)

Thomas Hoving served for ten exciting, turbulent years as director of the Met. He was probably the most famous museum man in the world, and certainly the most controversial. He had a great flair for making news and for mounting fascinating shows. He brought thousands of people to the Met who had never before seen the inside of a museum. In my judgment, Hoving, more than any other single person, was responsible for the explosion in museum attendance we see today.

Before he became director of the Met, Hoving was a talented scholar of medieval art, working at the Met's medieval Cloisters in upper Manhattan.

He left the Met to be New York City parks commissioner for a short time in the administration of Mayor John Lindsay. In this capacity, he revolutionized the use of Central Park by closing it to automobiles for part of the day, which made it more accessible to the public and demonstrated that the automobile was not the kingpin in Manhattan. A lot of people were angry about the closing because traffic got worse in some parts of the city. But most of what Hoving did for Central Park still prevails.

Tom was very young when he took over the Met. Early in his reign, he and I would have chats about events at the Met. I tried to be helpful.

Hoving is a combination of characters: He is a politician, he is very convincing when you are with him, as was Nelson Rockefeller, and he is extraordinarily bright and likeable. I have always liked him. He admitted to being a little arrogant at times. He did not get along with curators as well as James Rorimer, Sherman Lee, or Carter Brown.

Tom Hoving ushered in an era of great physical change at the Met. His master plan, approved by the board in 1970, called for doubling the size of the Met. He helped select the architects and worked closely with them. His plans are still being put into effect.

He also, in my view, made some bad judgment calls. Debates still rage about the vase he bought for the Greek and Roman department under peculiar circumstances, without a clear title. The price was $1 million—more than anyone had ever paid for a piece of ancient art. Previously, $250,000 was the absolute top price for that kind of art.

Hoving and the Velazquez Affair

One of the most controversial issues museums deal with is the occasional need to sell off some holdings. This goes on in every museum, usually rather quietly. Deacquisitioning is probably necessary because there's an awful lot of junk in most museums. But it should be done with great care. Tom Hoving brought the subject to the front pages with his debatable decision to sell a Vincent van Gogh, an Henri Rousseau, and some rare coins to buy a Velazquez.

He was determined to buy the portrait of *Juan de Pareja* by Diego Rodriguez Velazquez, which had been sought for the Met since the days of Francis Taylor and James Rorimer. Pareja, also a painter, was Velazquez's assistant. The well-known portrait is affectionate and brilliant. Apparently, it was the last remaining great Velazquez not in a museum. And it was very expensive.

The final cost was $5,440,000, at that time the highest price ever paid at an auction for a picture. By the end of the twentieth century, so many pictures were sold for over $50 million that it might be hard to realize what a fuss a payment of under $5.5 million had caused.

There were problems with the way Hoving went about this acquisition. He didn't tell the Trustees in advance that he was going to pay a huge price for it. In addition, his sale of the coins and paintings caused a huge ruckus. Some called it Hoving's Folly.

The Met did not have anywhere near $5.5 million available for new acquisitions. A famous painting today could go for up to $80 million, a van Gogh for instance. But at that time, Hoving couldn't raise the money. He asked for individual contributions. My recollection is that seven Trustees gave him $100,000 each. He was short almost $5 million. Then, instead of getting the Trustees further involved in raising the money to acquire the Velazquez, he quietly made the sales. Coin collectors were furious. Although coins aren't my thing, I recognize them as important collectibles. The paintings came from the Adelaide Milton de Groot collection. She was the lady who, at my house in 1944 with a committee from the Modern Museum, told a friend that her art collection was better than mine. I have always said that she was right. Adelaide Milton de Groot lived into her nineties. Every museum wanted her collection. She gave it all to the Metropolitan, including the van Gogh and Rousseau that Hoving sold to the Marlborough Gallery.

It was particularly unfortunate that the paintings were sold quite soon after her death. I think it would have been a mistake to sell her art at any time, but it was an even bigger mistake to sell it so quickly, without allowing a decent interval of time.

Hoving should not have sold the paintings. I feel it violated the trust of the collector, Mrs. de Groot. He shouldn't have sold the coins either. In other words, Hoving did not act the way the director of a great museum should act. As a result, this sale became a cause celebre. Public criticism was severe.

The van Gogh sale was not as bad as the Rousseau. The difference is not a question of quality. Though van Gogh lived a short life, he painted much more than Rousseau. The Met has several van Goghs, including one donated by Ambassador Walter Annenberg that was quite similar to the de Groot gift. But Henri Rousseau was a different matter. Rousseau, one of the great primitives of modern times, was a much less prolific artist. Rousseaus are so rare that you don't dispose of them lightly. The Met had only two Rousseaus, including the fine painting donated by Adelaide de Groot. The Modern has two and the Met should have two. The Velazquez *Juan de Pareja* is a fine painting, but there were other Velazquezes in New York. The Met has other Velazquezes. So does the Frick Collection.

I felt so strongly about this matter that I went to the Marlborough Gallery, without anyone knowing about it in advance, and asked, "If the Metropolitan wanted to get those pictures back, would you accommodate them?" They said yes, they would. I immediately called Douglas Dillon, who was then president of the Metropolitan Museum, and at lunch that day I told him about my trip to the Marlborough Gallery. Mr. Dillon listened attentively, but I never heard anything more about it.

I don't know what Douglas Dillon thought about the sale of the van Gogh and the Rousseau, but I have great respect for the affable Mr. Dillon. He has devoted his life to the public good. He played an important role in the extraordinary history of the Metropolitan. Major works at the Met could not be sold without the consent of the Trustees. I was at the Trustees' meeting when the issue of selling these two paintings came up. Usually, Trustees go along with the recommendations of the Director. If they like the Director and have confidence in him, policy questions are treated more as a report of what is happening than a request for permission. But in this case, there were people who really fought against what Tom was doing. In the end, the tradition of Trustees supporting decisions and actions of the Director won out.

I would never say that you should not purchase the work of a great artist, and certainly Velazquez is one of the greatest artists. Hoving wanted a really fine painting. But when you buy a painting, you have to have the money for it.

Some people feel that the Velazquez was a brilliant purchase. But there were other ways to do it. If he had been an English director trying to buy a great work, Hoving might have asked for a public subscription. It is what the National Gallery in London or the Tate might have done.

When the National Gallery in London wants a desirable work of art, like the fragment of a da Vinci which came on the market in the late twentieth century, they sponsor a public subscription. If the Met had advertised for wide participation in the purchase of the Velazquez, they could have raised the money they needed.

One of Hoving's many constructive innovations was to buy art in conjunction with other museums. The first such joint purchase was with the Louvre. It was an ancient piece, which alternates between the Louvre and the Met, bought for about $60,000.

Looking back—and I believe in looking back as educational for the future, not to second-guess others—if I knew as much then as I know now, I would have recommended that the Velazquez be purchased in partnership with one or two other museums of the calibre of the National Gallery in Washington or the Cleveland Museum of Art. Other museums were bidding for it. If there had been no active bidding on behalf of museums, the Velazquez might have gone for about $3 million. This would have meant $1 million each for three museums or a million and a half for two, and there would have been no great problem.

Bidding up to a very high price for this picture, the deacquisition of paintings, and other events in this uproar created something akin to Dukas' musical composition *The Sorcerer's Apprentice*, which demonstrates what can happen when something is set in motion and it goes on and on to its own destruction.

There must be a sense of cooperation between the great people who understand art. I'm sorry that there wasn't more cooperation among people like Tom Hoving and John Walker and Carter Brown and Sherman Lee at the Cleveland to work together, instead of competing, to acquire great works of art.

An important, long-term issue of the Velazquez debate was the question of how selling the two paintings and the rare coins might affect future gifts.

During the controversy, I was a luncheon guest of an important Trustee for wealthy families. He told me that after the sale of Adelaide de Groot's paintings, some gifts that were to go to the Metropolitan were taken out of the wills for those trusts.

The Met has the Velazquez. But it was a rocky road to the acquisition, and we will never know what was lost along the way.

Hoving in Perspective

In spite of such controversies, Tom Hoving was a strong, imaginative, and effective director of the Met. By bringing tremendous numbers of people to the museum, he showed that people are thirsty for knowledge about human history, which can be learned through the visual arts.

The Egyptian collection at the Met, for instance, is probably better than the collection at the Louvre, and even greater than the museum in Cairo. Through this immense collection, people who didn't think they had any interest in ancient Egypt become vitally involved in learning about a civilization many thousands of years old. The same happened with the Met's marvelous Greek collection, and is now happening with its refurbished Chinese galleries.

Hoving is a superb businessman, perhaps a better one than his father, who headed Tiffany. We like to think of Tiffany as the best of its kind, certainly a beautiful store. From a retail sales viewpoint, Tom's store at the Met was extraordinarily successful.

A tip from a Morgan Library booklet sticks with me—"Advice of an art historian: The surest way to learn about art is to study thousands of examples and to put your knowledge to the test with purchases." Tom Hoving could have read that. What he did was increase the number of examples that one can see at the Metropolitan Museum without going anywhere else. In the balance, Thomas Hoving was a fine director.

THE DE MONTEBELLO ERA (1978–   )

One reason I think the Met is greater than the Louvre and other museums is its educational program. It has taught millions of people. Other museums also educate, but the Met does it best, largely because Philippe de Montebello is the best.

Hoving's successor is one of the most outstanding museum directors in American history. I rank him at the very top, among the few truly great directors. We are all fortunate to have him lead this greatest of all museums. He runs the museum beautifully.

De Montebello was born in France and educated in the United States. Before becoming head of the Met, he spent four years as director of the Houston Museum of Fine Arts.

He was appointed director of the Met in 1978. Douglas Dillon, who had been the unpaid president, became chairman of the Board; and the Met appointed a full-time paid president. De Montebello originally opposed the idea of a paid president. He was concerned about whether his successor would be as strong as he is in the relationship.

Art museums in Chicago and Philadelphia tried having both a paid president and a director and ultimately dropped it. William Luers, a former diplomat, appointed full-time president of the Met in 1986, was a good argument for the position. He and de Montebello were both talented fund raisers, complementing each other. They made a good team.

De Montebello is not only a scholar, he is a great manager. When the Louvre was looking for a new director, de Montebello was offered the job. He didn't want it. He wanted to stay at the Met.

As director, de Montebello has won the respect and support of curators, trustees, and staff. He is conservative, aristocratic, hardworking, and committed to the Met. He sometimes views his audience as the cultural elite, those already knowledgeable about art. But number one on many tourist lists is a visit to the Met.

Under de Montebello's leadership, the Met appeals to a broad audience without sacrificing its relationship with an educated art elite. There are days when the Met is unbelievably crowded with busloads of suburbanites, schoolchildren, and out-of-town visitors, yet it still provides a haven for scholars and artists. Serving a disparate clientele is one of the things the Met does best.

The rebuilt gallery of ancient Greek art is an example of progress at the Met that pleases both the expert and a wider audience. Everyone is delighted with it. And the Asian collection has become so strong that the Met is now the largest museum of Asian art outside Asia.

Bill Lieberman, the Met's curator of twentieth-century art, came from MoMA. I know him well, and I think he is doing a fine job. Lieberman is a professional of long experience who has achieved a great deal at the Met. He spent many years at MoMA but became unhappy there after the death of the director, Rene d'Harnoncourt. At about the same time, Tom Hess, the Met's twentieth-century curator, died.

George Goldner, the Met's curator of drawings and prints, who came from the Getty Museum, was offered the job of director of the distinguished Ashmolean Museum in Oxford, England. He turned it down to stay at the Met, saying, "I think this is probably the best-managed museum in the world. There is more emphasis on excellence and on maintaining high standards of scholarship and design, and there is also a strangely egalitarian atmosphere in the way people are treated, which wasn't true at the Getty."

METROPOLITAN HONORARY LIFE TRUSTEE

In January 1968, I received a wonderful invitation. The Metropolitan Museum was establishing a new category called honorary life trustee. I was invited to occupy one of these positions. I have been awarded five honorary degrees, but being an honorary life trustee of the Met is much more important to me.

Arthur Houghton, a cousin of Alice Tully who was then president of the Met, set up these new positions: honorary life trustees were to be selected for their service to the Met and to art in general. As one of three people named the first honorary life trustees, I was flattered to be in the company of Professor Craig Smythe, the distinguished head of the New York University Institute of Fine Arts, and Millard Meiss, a brilliant medieval art scholar at Princeton.

At that time, it was alleged that there was some anti-semitism at the Met. But Millard Meiss was of Jewish lineage, as am I. Our appointments showed that by 1968 being Jewish was not much of a factor.

As honorary life trustee, I have virtually the same access to go in and out of the museum as employees have. I don't take advantage of it.

In May 1996, Kitty Carlisle Hart, former head of the New York State Commission on the Arts, a marvelous woman who has done a great deal for art in America, also became an honorary life trustee.

I admire Kitty enormously. The day of her first trustee meeting, I moved my name plate and put it next to hers, so that we would be seated next to each other. From that time on our friendship accelerated.

MONEY AT THE MET

At different times I have been asked, as a person versed in the financial world, to take a look at the Met's holdings. Shortly after he became director, and after I became an honorary life trustee, Tom Hoving asked me to study the museum's finances, giving me all the particulars from the previous eighteen years. I did so and advised him that the finances were a mess. The investments were much too conservative. The return was way below what it should have been. For a great institution, the Met's finances were woefully inadequate.

Thanks to the superb leadership of Philippe de Montebello, the Met's finances are now in remarkably good shape, robust and well-invested. The Met is now developing a strong endowment.

For more than a half century, I have been involved in every fund drive at the Met. I am participating in the early twenty-first century drive. John Rosenwald, a retired partner at Bear Stearns and an exceedingly nice man, is chairman of the fund-raising committee.

The goal has been raised from $400 million to $650 million. The amount I give is insignificant compared to some other donors. But I have a responsibility of my own, to the Neuberger Museum. At the Met, they are very appreciative of what I do give.

In January 2000, I made a second gift of $100,000 to the Director's Discretionary Fund for Acquisitions. I enjoy helping the Met buy art. This time, I left it to their judgment as to what to buy with my gift, rather than making a donation earmarked for specific purchases. They no longer suffer from a paucity of work by living artists.

One day I was walking up the grand staircase that rises from the center of the Met lobby. Viewing the wall plaques on the left, I saw, under the years MCMLXI-MCMLXVI (1961–1966), Georgia O'Keeffe, John D. Rockefeller III, Alice Tully, Richard and Dorothy Rodgers—and a fellow named Neuberger. It took me back to the moment as a young man when I first discovered that I lacked the talent to paint well. Now, walking up the Met staircase, seeing my name in such company, I felt lucky and happy that I had been able to help those who did have the genius to create great art.

CONTEMPORARY ART AT THE MET

Rorimer and Hoving were both reluctant to commit the Met to any major involvement with art of the twentieth century. They felt that with three other museums in New York devoted to contemporary art (the Museum of Modern Art, the Whitney, and the Guggenheim), there was no compelling need for a major effort by the Met. De Montebello was also not overly receptive to modern art, yet he was the one who did the most for it. Under his stewardship, the Met established the Henry R. Kravis Wing for European Sculpture and Decorative Arts and the Lila Acheson Wallace Wing for Twentieth-Century Art.

There was a pragmatic reason for de Montebello to devote attention and resources to contemporary art. Many collectors focus on recent art because that is what's available for them to buy. It became clear that if the Met wanted to attract support from these collectors, it had to provide space where their collections could be seen to their best advantage.

Art is always modern at the time it is done. The Renaissance was modern art in its day and its great artists were modern in their time.

By now, I think the Met has a pretty good collection of our time. I am glad my efforts resulted in some splendid artists being represented, but there is a bit of controversy about it. Some people feel that the contemporary collection is too much. It *is* large, occupying parts of three floors.

The Met doesn't have to reflect what is going on in the art world at this moment, collecting what is happening up-to-the minute. That is not its job. In its attention to modern art, as to every other period of art, the Met should concern itself with what is of lasting artistic value.

The Metropolitan was always interested in contemporary art, but erratic about it. Special space for contemporary art was not set aside until late in the twentieth century. Today, I believe the Metropolitan's collection of twentieth-century art is a solid, impressive representation of art in America and around the world.

Roy Neuberger, Nelson Rockefeller, and Philip Johnson look over the model for Neuberger Museum. (Photo by Myles Aronowitz.)

CHAPTER EIGHT

THE NEUBERGER MUSEUM OF ART

Like most art museums, the Neuberger Museum of Art has basement storage areas containing thousands of works of art. In November 2001, museum director Lucinda Gedeon and I began going through these paintings, many from my collection. I frequently bought artists who were unknown or little known at the time I acquired their work. Many of them are winners whose art is displayed in our second floor permanent gallery or is out on loan to other museums. But the judgment of time renders some, though not terrible pictures, undistinguished. I don't want to keep anything that is not distinguished.

As we deliberated many hours, reviewing the merits of each work, my mind went back to 1965 when I received an anonymous offer of $6 million for my collection. Later, I learned that the offer had come from Governor Nelson Rockefeller. I turned it down because I exhibit art, I loan it, I give much of it away, but I do not sell the work of a living artist.

Ultimately, Governor Rockefeller approached me directly. With respect to my collection, he said, "Give it to me." By "me" he meant the State of New York. In May 1967, Rockefeller offered to create a Neuberger Museum to house my collection. It would be built on the Purchase College campus of the State University in Westchester County near New York City.

When Governor Rockefeller first approached me, the State University at Purchase didn't exist. It was one of many ideas bubbling inside Nelson Rockefeller's adventurous mind.

He broached the idea over lunch at Pocantico Hills, the huge Rockefeller family estate overlooking the Hudson River. I told him I would think about it. A few days later, I received an urgent invitation for cocktails at his Fifth Avenue apartment. Present were Governor Rockefeller, Chancellor Samuel Gould of the State University of New York, and Abbott Kaplan, who would be the first president of the new Purchase College.

Nelson Rockefeller slowly sipped a Dubonnet on the rocks as he expanded on the proposal. On the strength of a martini or two, I became enamored of his inspiring description not only of the museum-to-be but also of the entire campus-to-be. I agreed to give the museum a substantial portion of the collection I had at the time, over 300 items. (Ultimately, I gave the Neuberger more than 950 paintings and sculptures as well as money for purchases.)

I doubt if anyone but Nelson Rockefeller could get a contrarian like me to part with more than $5 million worth of art (at that time the largest single gift in SUNY history) on the strength of two meetings, but Nelson was one of the most vibrant and persuasive characters that ever lived. I ended up respecting and liking him.

Governor Rockefeller and Chancellor Gould envisioned the Purchase College campus as both an institution of higher education and an arts and cultural center, a miniature Lincoln Center with an opera house and theaters, serving communities in New York and Connecticut.

I am ambivalent about some aspects of the campus. The buildings were designed by splendid architects. Like the Neuberger Museum, they are terrific inside. But outside, they are lumped together like a pile of bricks. The effect is somewhat bleak and crowded—unnecessarily so, for the college is situated on 500 acres of beautiful land.

Hopefully, Nelson's inspiration for Purchase College was well-founded and eventually the campus, devoted to the best things in life—the arts, the humanities, and culture—will live up to his expectations.

Some Rockefeller projects pay off in the very long run, but not necessarily in the short run. Rockefeller Center was an exception. It was wonderful immediately and still is a marvelous focal point for tourists and for New Yorkers. When I walk past the ice skating rink I feel a little of Vienna in the middle of New York. Millions of people come to Rockefeller Center every year. It is a wonderful use of urban space. Each time I see it, I feel a great sense of pride as a New Yorker.

Nelson Rockefeller brought to New York State government, during his fifteen years in office, the same kind of romantic vision that led to the creation of Rockefeller Center. He focused much attention on building institutions of higher education. California has an older and still stronger system, but Rockefeller quickly put a quality State University of New York on the map.

With the same kind of enthusiasm, he persuaded me that my collection was large enough and important enough so that the New York State legislature would agree to build a museum to house it.

BUILDING THE NEUBERGER MUSEUM

Our agreement was relatively simple, but the process moved so slowly through the bureaucracy that it was two years before we signed the final document.

For one who trades thousands of securities with the flick of a button, it tried my patience to wait two years to execute something I had already agreed to. But *finally*, in the fall of 1969, we signed all the papers, standing in front of the Edward Hopper painting, *Barber Shop*, which the *New York Times* photographer wanted in the background.

We agreed that the renowned architect Philip Johnson, who has probably built more museums than anyone else in history, would design the Neuberger Museum, and that I would give the museum most of my art. Of course, I could not give them what I had already given to seventy other institutions. It was also understood that I had homes and an office where art was displayed. But most of what I had would go to the museum.

As soon as I saw Philip Johnson's plans, I knew he would create a jewel. Johnson had been the first director of the Department of Architecture at the Museum of Modern Art. To my mind, his aesthetic feelings about this new museum were perfect.

The Neuberger Museum of Art was the first building to be completed on the new Purchase College campus. While other buildings were under construction, we provided space for a library and classrooms, art studios, and dance labs. We held our official opening, a festive affair, in May 1974, featuring not only my collection but the George and Edith Rickey Collection of Constructivist Art and the Malsin Collection of the art of New Guinea.

I feel that the building itself is a sculpture. You might call the Guggenheim Museum on Fifth Avenue in New York City a sculpture by Frank Lloyd Wright. The Neuberger Museum of Art is a sculpture by Philip Johnson.

It is also more than ample spatially for many simultaneous exhibits. Gibson Danes, Purchase College's first dean of Arts and Architecture, told me that the museum is longer and wider than a football field.

The interior is brilliant, simple, and efficient. It gives the art an opportunity to breathe. The first floor is an enormous open space divided into separate galleries and outdoor courtyards so we can handle several different shows at the same time, and also host dinners and receptions.

One room was designed to be a real challenge to artists. It is 22-feet high and has 5,000 square feet. The challenge to fill the walls was first taken up in 1974 by Cleve Gray, who did a Herculean job painting fourteen panels that appear to be one. The monumental *Threnody*, shown again in 2002, creates a marvelous environment.

The second floor houses pictures and sculptures from my collection, including works by Jackson Pollock, Georgia O'Keeffe, Edward Hopper, and of course, many Milton Averys. The skylights on the second and third floors bring in a great deal of light. The whole museum has the feeling and the reality of open space with natural lighting.

I am particularly fond of the sculpture areas, that include a terrific Alexander Lieberman, a George Rickey—a real joy that I bought soon after the museum opened—and the rather whimsical red, yellow, and black Calder mobile (*The Red Ear*) hanging over the open stairway to the second floor.

OUR HENRY MOORE SCULPTURE

While the Neuberger Museum was being built, Henry Moore gave us an abstract sculpture 20 feet high and 29 feet wide, weighing seven and a half tons, called *Large Two Forms*. It is a magnificent piece of work and one of the biggest sculptures Moore ever created. I like it better than the Moore outside of Lincoln Center. Henry donated the sculpture as a gift to the museum.

He created the sculpture in England but planned to cast it in Germany. He told me, "If you help pay for the casting, you can have it." Because of the size of the sculpture, the casting cost $125,000.

I paid about $89,000 and Henry generously paid the rest. We then put *Large Two Forms* on a ship for the voyage across the Atlantic, which cost another $13,000. Finally, it was trucked up to the Purchase campus.

The sculpture was placed during the final days of construction, just before the official opening of the museum. Because of its extreme weight, it couldn't be placed just anywhere; it had to be placed on solid ground. Also, its size demanded an important base. It sits about an eighth of a mile from the museum, but it belongs to the museum. I tried to get it moved, but it is too heavy.

I am a bit irritated that this important piece was placed so far from the museum, at the extreme end of a complex of campus buildings. I am not alone in this feeling. Many of us are unhappy about it.

There is a book about *Large Two Forms*, consisting mostly of photographs, all of this one work, taken from different angles. The photographer, David Finn, is more that just an enthusiast for Moore, he is a fanatic. Taken from multiple angles, the sculpture looks very different in each photograph.

POPULAR PICTURES AT THE MUSEUM

I enjoy watching people look at the art I have collected. It reminds me of when I first looked at those same paintings and sculptures.

The Jackson Pollock, *Number 8, 1949*, attracts a lot of attention. After I first saw it at the Betty Parsons Gallery, I couldn't get it out of my mind. I think it is one of Pollock's finest paintings, matched only by *Autumn Rhythm* at the Metropolitan and *The One* at the Museum of Modern Art. Buying it was one of the best decisions I ever made.

Edward Hopper's *Barber Shop*, another hugely popular picture, is one of the finest of Hopper's portrayals of America. He painted it in 1931 during one of the worst years of the depression.

Both the Hopper and the Pollock have been exhibited throughout America and in many international shows.

When, in the early 1950s, I finally decided I wanted a Hopper for my collection, and started looking for a great example of his work, it was fairly late in his career. Museums and other collectors had already acquired the best.

One day, I went into the Rehn Gallery, which at that time was run by a fellow named John Clancey. I asked him, "John, can you get me a great Hopper?"

He said, "I can think of only one great Hopper. It is in Mr. Hopper's home in Truro, on Cape Cod in Massachusetts."

Fortunately, Edward Hopper agreed that it would be nice to be included in my collection. He took the painting off the wall and sold it to me for a very fair price. I liked it so much that I would have been happy to buy it at double the price.

Another favorite is Richard Diebenkorn's *Girl on a Terrace*, which I acquired in 1957. It is a painting to which I return again and again, by an artist of remarkable talent. I like the color, the composition, the scale, and the fact that it contains a human image, something I discovered I missed during a long exposure to totally abstract works. People must agree with me because this painting has attracted a great deal of attention during its years at the Neuberger.

A popular work is *Melon Season*, Romare Bearden's colorful, appealing painting that I bought in 1967 from the Cordier & Ekstrom Gallery, even though I don't like watermelon.

One of the best-known paintings in my collection is the Willem de Kooning portrait of Marilyn Monroe. It is famous partly because of de Kooning, partly because of Marilyn. I got so used to the painting that I thought I knew her, but I didn't.

In 1955, in a gallery backroom just before the official opening of a de Kooning exhibit, I was shown a number of de Koonings by an extraordinary dealer, a woman originally from Buffalo, Martha Jackson. Her gallery was on Sixty-ninth Street and Broadway.

I was interested in acquiring a de Kooning figurative painting. As soon as I saw *Marilyn* I knew this was the painting. I guess my choice was influenced in part because I thought Marilyn Monroe was quite a woman. I felt that de Kooning had interpreted her with a gentleness not found in other depictions of her, and this had great appeal to me. The painting seems to evoke a strong emotional response in everyone who sees it. It is one of the pictures most requested for loans to shows at other museums.

Still, some artists become more famous than perhaps they should be. Maybe de Kooning wasn't quite as good as his fame would indicate. We can't say for sure.

Ben Shahn's *The Blind Accordion Player*, Georgia O'Keeffe's *Lake George by Early Moonrise*, and paintings by Milton Avery are other works in the Neuberger with strong appeal to viewers.

Max Weber's *La Parisienne 1907* should be one of the most popular attractions, but I am not sure it is. It has very much the quality of a Matisse, with whom he was studying at that time.

Admirers of the Hudson River School find in the museum the group's famous founder, Thomas Cole. Cole's *The Voyage of Life: Old Age*, about 1840, is an extremely good oil sketch, painted shortly before the final version. In many ways, it is better than the final painting that is owned by the National Gallery.

THE MUSEUM'S LEADERSHIP

With one long-ago exception, we have had excellent, high-quality directors at the museum, none better than our current director Lucinda

Gedeon, a thoroughly knowledgeable professional, a champion of new artists, a community cheer leader, and a master at fund-raising who has served since 1991.

Under Lucinda's leadership, the museum has mounted several important exhibitions every year and has sent a number of retrospectives, including Marisol, Mary Frank, and the great African American artist Elizabeth Catlett, to other museums around the country.

The Neuberger Museum is a public-private partnership. The state owns the land and the building and provides one-third of the staff and some maintenance. Everything else at the museum is funded by our endowment fund and enthusiastic Friends of the Neuberger Museum, originally formed to support outreach to the community. Over the years, the Friends have raised money for educational programs and many special events.

Support by the Friends has been crucial to our educational and travel programs, public lectures, symposia, musical events, visits to homes with great art, and receptions honoring the artists. We also host the youth of the region, who come to the museum in large numbers from schools throughout the area.

Some of my family and friends are active with the Friends and have made important additions to the collection. My partner Philip Straus gave a painting by Alexi Jawlensky and another partner, Howard Lipman, even though he was president of the Whitney Museum, donated a number of excellent sculptures to the Neuberger. George Rickey, himself a great sculptor, made major contributions from his collection of constructivist art, and Philip Johnson contributed paintings from his substantial collection.

Through the generous gifts of many in the community, the museum's collection has grown to more than 6,000 works of art.

Bryan Robertson, the noted critic and curator, was appointed the first director of the museum. He had been the influential director of the Whitechapel Art Gallery in London, where he was the first to introduce Jackson Pollock and other contemporary American painters to British art lovers. It was said that Robertson taught Britain to love modern art.

We have nearly always been fortunate in our choice of directors of the Neuberger Museum. One early director, however, emboldened by the enormous space in the basement, became involved in running a private art gallery down there. He left quickly when this misuse of a public facility was discovered.

While we searched for a replacement, we were lucky to have as interim director Professor Irving Sandler, a lovely man and a brilliant art historian, a teacher, and a superb writer. Our search for a permanent director ended with Suzanne Delehanty, who had been director of the Institute of Contemporary Art at the University of Pennsylvania, and was part of the growing focus on the development of contemporary art in museums around the country.

During her nine years at the helm of the Neuberger, the museum's collection grew substantially. We were able to buy art because the Friends, as our acquisition committee, raised funds to enhance and broaden the collection. They still do a wonderful job.

But the state is a terrible landlord, bad at keeping up the property. Money that we might have used to acquire new art has had to go instead into upkeep of the museum.

As he promised, Governor Rockefeller built a wonderful building. However, money he assured us would be forthcoming, from him personally for art and from the state for maintenance, has never appeared.

MAJOR EXHIBITIONS AT THE MUSEUM

When Nelson Rockefeller and I were working out the details of setting up the museum, he asked me, "Do you want this museum for yourself alone? It will be that way if you want it."

I said, "No. I do not. I want it to be broader than that. It will be a much better museum if it is open-ended." I think time has vindicated that opinion.

Over more than a quarter of a century, we have hosted important exhibitions of many of the world's great artists, including David Smith, Alexander Calder, George Segal, Helen Frankenthaler, and Marisol, who several years ago showed an enormous work at the Met, *The Last Supper*. Marisol is truly a sculptor to be reckoned with. Her early wood and terracotta sculpture, *Queen*, which I bought in 1957 when she was in her twenties, always has been a favorite of mine. It is still in my apartment.

The 1978 Louise Nevelson exhibit was a major event at the Neuberger. It included large welded metal pieces, not the wood sculptures usually identified with Nevelson.

Louise Nevelson was definitely a hands-on sculptor. Casting was done at a local foundry. She spent days at the museum closely supervising the installation. It was a great time for our staff. She worked in the gallery all day and had lunch with them in the museum's outdoor courtyard.

Opening night of the Nevelson exhibit featured ninety-two dinner parties in homes, apartments, and penthouses throughout Westchester, New York City, and Connecticut. After dinner, 2,000 people came together at the museum for a champagne and dessert reception. I was told that if you were in the New York area that night, the museum was *the* place to be. It was a magical evening that people are still talking about.

A little less celebrated but quite interesting exhibit, I thought, was "Edward Albee/Roy Neuberger Select," which showed art I chose from the dramatist Edward Albee's collection, and works from my collection selected by Mr. Albee. He has a collection similar to mine, focusing on works of living artists. It was a very popular show.

A great show at the Neuberger in the fall of 2001 featured paintings by Grace Hartigan, whose work I bought in 1955, when she was at her very best. *Gift Wares* shows her luscious paint quality and strong composition. It belongs to the Neuberger now.

Although Grace Hartigan was not well in October 2001, when we had a big party honoring her, she got up and spoke. She said I had helped her develop confidence in herself because I was one of the earliest purchasers of her work. I was pleased to have it confirmed that my work in buying artists early in their careers was good for the artists. That is what I had set out to do, so it was heartwarming to hear her say that I had succeeded.

Mary Frank, a leading contemporary artist, first showed seventy-five sculptures in an exhibit at the Neuberger in the late 1970s and then switched to painting. We showed her paintings in 2000. She is not just very good; she is terrific.

In 2001, Lawrence Gussman gave the major portion of his important African collections to the Neuberger. These 140 exceptionally fine examples of African art were introduced at a major exhibition. They are among the significant additions beyond my own core collection, in keeping with my conversation with Governor Rockefeller.

Unlike the Met, the Neuberger is not encyclopedic. Our strengths are in modern, contemporary, and now African art.

Reviewing the history of the Neuberger Museum, I am grateful to Governor Rockefeller for suggesting it, to Philip Johnson for designing it, to the State of New York for building it, to our terrific director and staff who each day bring it to life, and to the thousands of visitors who enjoy it, confirming my judgment that the twentieth century produced brilliant, adventurous, groundbreaking artists whose work will be valued through the ages.

Roy Neuberger in front of Paul George's *Kaldis at the Cedar Street Bar,* 1966. (Photo by Myles Aronowitz.)

CHAPTER NINE

ADVICE FOR YOUNG
(UNDER NINETY-NINE) COLLECTORS

A person who collects art in quantity has to be a little bit nuts. I started giving away art because I felt strongly that I was only borrowing it. I believe you must give in this world, either money or art or spirit. You must give something.

I have tried to influence thousands of people to relate to art. By nature, I am a salesperson and the principal thing I have sold is that the arts are a way of life.

I hope that sharing my adventures as a passionate collector will encourage you to begin collecting at your own pace and on your own scale.

You will have the opportunity to learn from artists, dealers, scholars, and museum leaders—an exciting group of people.

I am pleased to offer you ten basic principles of collecting. These are the fundamentals that have guided me. They still apply today.

1. *Take a deep breath.* Do you really want to do this? You should have a natural love of the visual arts. If you don't have the passion, you can still buy well, but it won't be as much fun.

Some people collect to enhance their social standing. But you don't have to be a millionaire to build a collection. A recent example is a postal worker who became an eminent collector and gave a big gift to the National Gallery.

You won't be surprised to know that I hope you will want to buy art and ultimately give it away to enhance the artist's reputation and the public's enjoyment.

Some collect art for their own personal pleasure, sharing their collection with family and friends but not necessarily the public. Or you may start building a collection primarily as an appreciating investment. That's fine. It still helps the artists. And in a time of extreme volatility in the markets, art has proven to be a sound investment.

In the early days, Milton Avery's paintings were not highly valued. When I began buying Averys, people didn't like them. Giving away his paintings did nothing for me from a tax standpoint. Now he is one of the most popular twentieth-century painters. Since the mid-1970s, giving away paintings has helped me with taxes. But I would have profited more by selling them, which I never did.

2. *Study art history.* You can't begin in a vacuum—or without a foundation. I have never forgotten my classes with the legendary Walter Pach at the Sorbonne during the years I lived in Paris. While listening to that brilliant teacher, I first began to think about collecting.

Pach is no longer around. Nor is my old Paris friend, the great Columbia art historian Meyer Schapiro. But Columbia still has a great art history department. So do Cooper Union and the New York University Institute of Fine Arts. A number of art history professors teach in Columbia's School of General Studies, where adults can study part-time. Excellent courses are also offered at Purchase College, Harvard, Yale, Princeton, the University of Michigan, Berkeley, Stanford, UCLA, and other distinguished colleges and universities.

Museums where wonderful courses are available include the Metropolitan, the Brooklyn Museum, the Morgan Library, the Art Institute of Chicago, the Getty Museum (both the new Getty in Los Angeles and the old Getty in Malibu) and, of course, many others around the country.

3. *Read widely.* In addition to taking courses, read widely about art on your own. The more you know, the better you will be at developing your own point of view. Read books, magazines, catalogues, and reviews.

I learned an enormous amount in my early years from reading Bernard Berenson, Clive Bell, Roger Fry, and George Moore, as well as Meyer Schapiro. I have kept reading about art for the past eighty years.

Biographies of artists can enhance your appreciation of their work. Floret Fels' *Vincent van Gogh* did even more than that for me. It opened my eyes to the terrible indifference of the public to the poverty, hunger, and despair that mark the struggle of many artists just to survive in order to pursue their work.

4. *Visit museums and galleries frequently.* Lectures and books are useful. But the vital center of art education is looking at art.

You will discover visually what the world considers to be great art. In the process, you will learn what you yourself like. The two may not necessarily be the same. Without doing your own research first-hand, you will never know.

As a young man, I was lucky to have coworkers at B. Altman who introduced me to art galleries that I would never have gone to on my own. By the time I reached Paris, I needed no encouragement to hang out in the Louvre, the Luxembourg, the Jeu de Paumes (forerunner of the Musee D'Orsay), and later in Florence at the Uffizi. If I were still traveling, I would love to go back to those museums, as well as to the National Gallery in London, the Prado in Madrid, the Hermitage in St. Petersburg, and the Ashmolean Museum in Oxford.

Our country has magnificent museums, including the world's finest—the Metropolitan. I also go occasionally to the Whitney, the Frick, the Guggenheim, MoMA, the Morgan Library, the Brooklyn Museum, and the other great museums in New York City, and of course, frequently to the Neuberger Museum of Art in Westchester.

Our nation's capital has splendid museums—the National Gallery and other parts of the Smithsonian, the Phillips Collection, and the Corcoran Gallery of Art.

America also has an abundance of small museums, from the Montclair Museum in New Jersey, to the Butler Institute of American Art in Youngstown, Ohio.

We have great museums in unlikely places, like the Wadsworth Atheneum in Hartford, Connecticut; the Worcester Art Museum; the Barnes Museum in Merion, Pennsylvania; the Norton Simon Museum in Pasadena, California; and the Munson-Williams-Proctor Institute in Utica, New York.

Every major city in the United States has a museum worth visiting, including the Albright-Knox Art Gallery in Buffalo; the Institute of Fine Arts in Chicago; the Walker Art Center in Minneapolis; the Atkins Museum of Fine Arts in Kansas City; the Cleveland Art Institute; the Boston Museum of Fine Arts and the Gardner Museum, also in Boston; in Houston, the Museum of Fine Arts, the De Menil Collection, and Bayou Bend; the Philadelphia Museum of Art; the Baltimore Museum of Art, and the Walters Art Gallery, also in Baltimore; and many more.

Art galleries are all over New York, from Madison Avenue and the Fifties to Greenwich Village, SoHo, Tribeca, and Chelsea—

everywhere. Some of the galleries where I made purchases long ago, like the Sidney Janis Gallery, the Leo Castelli Gallery and the ACA Gallery, are still in existence and are still fine galleries. Some of the more recent galleries, like the Maxwell Davidson Gallery, show the kind of art I would buy if I were still collecting.

When I visit Santa Fe, I can go to 250 galleries in one compact community.

5. *Listen to advice—but make your own decision.* To whatever degree you develop your knowledge and taste, you can always profit from the judgment of those who know more about art than you and I will ever know. That includes art historians and museum curators who, increasingly, are drawn from the ranks of university scholars. Dealers are sometimes the most knowledgeable and helpful of all.

You will probably learn less from other collectors because their personal preferences might be quite different than yours. Some of my fellow art collectors are my friends but not my advisors.

I have found that the artists themselves can be excellent critics— not necessarily of their own work. But they can be very smart about the work of other artists. The artist Jack Levine, who painted two of my favorites, *The Banquet* and *The Black Freighter*, made excellent recommendations to me in the mid-1970s and beyond.

6. *Buy unknowns.* This is perhaps the most important piece of advice I can give you. It requires a lot of leg work and eye work, but you get a better run for your money.

If you begin by buying well-known artists, you will be paying top dollar, you will be assisting an artist who may not need your assistance—or, more often, not even helping the artist but enriching a dealer or another collector—and you will miss the true adventure of collecting, which is discovery.

It is tempting to avoid that adventure because the eye is sold a bill of goods by the constant seeing of a reproduction of a well-known painting. If it is a great painting, it becomes even greater. (This may be true of some of Picasso's paintings.) If it is a poor painting, it sometimes gets more attention than it should have, and it becomes famous.

7. *Be wary of fads.* They are like stocks that shoot up quickly and then plummet.

When the Impressionists were alive, their work was castigated. At auctions in the 1990s, Van Gogh and Monet sold for millions. Now some critics dismiss their work as too pretty.

There is no question that Andrew Warhol has lasted longer than 15 minutes. As a result of recent auction sales, his work is valued at an all-time high. But I wonder if he or Mark Rothko will endure.

8. *Buy what you like.* Art should arouse your own personal emotions, a very individual matter. For example, I would probably not like to own the works of two English artists who are no longer unknown, but today are very famous and expensive—Francis Bacon and Lucien Freud. They are terrific for someone else, just not my cup of tea. Taste in art is not only very individual, it also changes as time goes by and you learn more.

Some artists I like better than others, but I don't have a favorite, not even two or three favorites. To me that is small thinking.

I am very fond of all the paintings you see in this book. Most of them I liked even more as I got to know them over the years. At no time did I buy a painting by an unknown artist that I didn't like but thought it would one day be valuable. That would take the fun out of collecting. You may as well trade in precious metals.

9. *Buy the best.* Whether it is a potentially great artist or an already recognized artist, you should zero in on the best work. Even the finest artists produce some second-rate work. Don't buy it simply to include a famous name in your collection.

For example, when I decided to purchase works by Marsden Hartley, I sought his best, and found one of the greatest of American paintings, *Fishermen's Last Supper.* I applied the same principle to Lyonel Feininger, Arthur Dove, Jackson Pollock, Georgia O'Keeffe, and others.

It can be difficult identifying an artist's greatest work. In the case of Edward Hopper, I looked a long time before I found *Barber Shop*, which I believe is equal to his very best.

A corollary rule, which I have silently observed over the years, is useful when you are considering whether to buy an artist's work for the second time: Buy another one only if it is better than the original one. I don't know if that is necessarily a good rule or a bad one, but it keeps you and the artist on the upward path.

10. *Enjoy!* If you don't, you're in the wrong game.

It has been said that committed collectors continue to buy art when all of their walls are filled. That's me. Maybe it will be you too.

ABOUT THE CONNABLES

Alfred and Roma Connable, who assisted their friend Roy Neuberger in the preparation of his memoirs, are graduates of the University of Michigan, where they met while working on the college newspaper. They reside on Long Island, New York, and have two sons (Ben, a Marine Corps officer in the Middle East, and Joel, a television news reporter in Los Angeles). The Connables have been marriage and writing partners for 40 years.

INDEX